THE ANATOMY

GW00506688

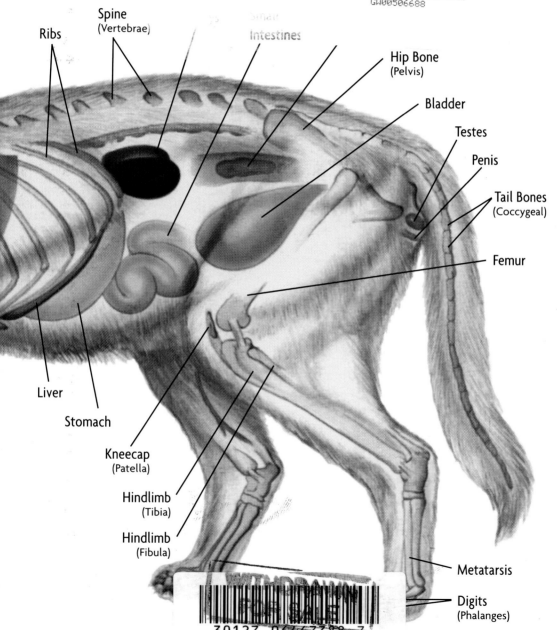

Ribs

Spine
(Vertebrae)

Small
Intestines

Hip Bone
(Pelvis)

Bladder

Testes

Penis

Tail Bones
(Coccygeal)

Femur

Liver

Stomach

Kneecap
(Patella)

Hindlimb
(Tibia)

Hindlimb
(Fibula)

Metatarsis

Digits
(Phalanges)

30127 06467388 7

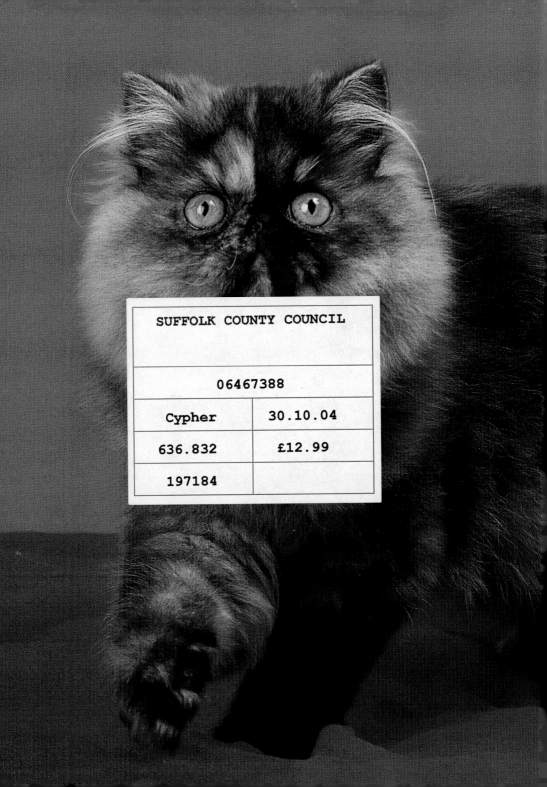

Persian Cat

By Thomas Critchley

Contents

PUBLISHED IN THE UNITED KINGDOM BY:

INTERPET
PUBLISHING

Vincent Lane, Dorking   Surrey RH4 3YX   England

ISBN 1-84286-007-0

All rights reserved.
No part of this book may be reproduced in any form, by photostat, scanner, microfilm, xerography or any other means, or incorporated into any information retrieval system, electronic or mechanical, without the written permission of the copyright owner.

Copyright © 2001 Animalia Books S. L.   Cover patent pending. Printed in Korea.

PHOTO CREDITS:
Photos by Isabelle Francais and Erin Winters
with additional photos provided by
Michael W. Brim, Cat Fanciers' Association, Carolina Biological Society, Fleabusters Rx for fleas, James R Hayden, RPB, Interpet, Dwight R Kuhn, Dr Dennis Kunkel, Phototake, Jean Claude Revy, W.B. Saunders Company.
Illustrations by Renée Low.

The publisher wishes to thank Laura Cure, Chris Gilman, Faye and Maurice LaValley, Dr Gail Lichten, Pat Marengo, Louise Panfile, Suzanne Suraci-Pellegrini, and the rest of the owners of dogs featured in this book.

Tracing the full history of the Persian will always remain an impossible task. As a researcher moves steadily backwards in time, the landmarks—points of clear reference—become fewer and more obscure. Eventually there is nothing. History is lost in the sands of the deserts from which this magnificent breed may first have emerged.

Of necessity this chapter can only be brief. However, it is hoped it will give the reader a sound overview of the Persian's history. It is probable the first longhaired cats were the result of a spontaneous mutation that was retained as being novel, thus valuable to the cat's owner. Where this mutation occurred is not known, but it has been subject to speculation. The three favoured areas are the Middle East, Asia Minor and Russia.

A good choice would be within a circle that embraced southern Georgia, Armenia, Azerbaijan and northern Persia (now Iran). This would favour the spread of longhaired felines in all directions. As to when this mutation occurred, the best that can be done is to take a calculated guess based on what references, written or artistic, have so far

TURKISH TIES

You may wonder why there are many references to Turkish cats in this and other works on Persians. The reason is there were probably more of them than Persians. There is little doubt that the two types were indiscriminately interbred so as to make any clear distinctions debatable. The Persians and Angoras of the 17th and 18th centuries were probably quite similar. The Persian may have had a somewhat heavier body, but there is no indication that either of them had the denser fur. The history of the Persian, once it arrived in Europe, is therefore intrinsically bound with that of the Angora.

been unearthed. Using these as the guide, it would seem unlikely that longhaired cats existed much before the 16th century. Some authors have stated earlier dates but never cite the sources of their reference. A distinction must be made between legend, myths, hearsay, and realistic evidence.

THE PERSIAN IN EUROPE

Our knowledge of the arrival of Turkish/Persian cats into Europe is largely drawn from two noted scholars. Pietro della Valle (1586–1652) was an Italian nobleman. From 1614–26 he undertook a journey that would take him from Venice to India, via Turkey and Persia. During his stay in Isfahan, then the capital of Persia, he encountered cats that greatly impressed him.

He describes them as being of good size and longhaired, especially around the neck and on the tail—on which he said the hair was 6 inches long. He describes the coat as silky, lustrous and of a blue-grey colour. He acquired four pairs. These were sent to Rome via Naples. They are thought to have arrived in 1621.

The second famous reference is Nicolas-Claude Fabri de Pieresc (1580–1637). Fabri was well known throughout Europe as a

A lovely white Persian is so attractive; it is easy to see why people fall in love with longhaired cats.

scientist. Although not initially a cat-lover, he became one. He is regarded as being the first person to import Angora cats from Turkey into France. The exact date appears unknown, but it was very probably during the first quarter of the 17th century.

His biographer, Pierre Gassendi, tells us, 'He procured out of the East, Ash coloured, Dun, and Speckled Cats, beautiful to behold.' It is from Fabri that the notorious Cardinal de Richelieu obtained his Turkish cats. It can be assumed that Fabri had considerable influence on the spread of longhaired cats in Europe, more so than della Valle did.

It is likely that other imports arrived into Europe from both Turkey and Persia as the 17th century progressed. It is known that during 1699 a female named Brinbelle was sent from Constantinople (now Istanbul). The pedigrees of her offspring were recorded in the first book (now a classic) written on domestic cats. The author was a passionate cat-lover named Francois-Augustin Paradise de Moncrif (1687–1770).

His book, entitled *Histoire de Chats*, was published in Paris in 1727. In his work, Moncrif made an error in stating that Valle's cats arrived in Rome during 1521.

This may be why many later authors quote that date for the

THE CRYSTAL PALACE SHOW

On 13 July 1871, an event took place that changed the world of the domestic cat. In the Crystal Palace at Sydenham, London, the world's first all-breed cat show took place. It was organised by Harrison Weir (1824–1906), a noted animal artist and great lover of British Shorthairs.

The success of the cat show saw Weir become a noted cat judge and author. Today he is regarded as the 'father of the cat fancy.' In his later years he complained that Eastern cats were causing the demise of his beloved British Shorthairs. This did not endear him to Persian owners whose cats were now beginning to dominate the hobby.

Harrison Weir

The Crystal Palace show attracted thousands of people, many of whom had never seen, or were even aware of, some of the breed types. On display were many British Shorthairs, Siamese, Manx and a wild cat. Also present was a cat reputed to be direct from Persia. It was said to have a delightful personality and its colour was black, grey and white. White Persians were also on view. For many visitors these were by far the most impressive exhibits with their pale blue eyes and flowing fur.

arrival of Turkish and Persian cats in Europe. Some years later, George-Louis Leclerc Comte de Buffon (1707–1788) referred to the Eastern cats in his epic 44-volume set *Histoire Naturelle*. Leclerc had little regard for cats. He repeated Moncrif's date of 1521 for the arrival of longhaired cats into Europe.

As to what the original cats looked like, we cannot be sure. The descriptions given by Valle and Pieresc are hardly detailed. It should be remembered that throughout this early period the cats in Europe were being persecuted as the familiars of witches. It is fortunate for Eastern cats that many of the nobility favoured them. However, unlike dogs and horses, the cat was not deemed to be worthy of inclusion in family portraits.

During the 18th century this began to change. A number of excellent paintings featuring Eastern cats began to appear. One by Jean-Jacques Bachelier (c1761) features a white cat displaying a beautiful long coat. Its graceful body is immediately comparable to that of present-day Angoras. Another fine work is by Martin

Opposite page: The history of the Persian cat is intrinsically bound with that of the Turkish Angora, shown here.

THE DARLING OF THE ARISTOCRACY

By the turn of the 20th century, the Persian was already swamping the longhaired cat scene. A factor that had considerable influence on this was that Queen Victoria had owned Persians for some years. Another royal, Princess Victoria of Schleswig-Holstein was a breeder of chinchilla and blue Persians. The Persian was therefore the darling of the aristocracy. Its gorgeous long coat was making it the favourite cat for the exhibitor breeder, as well as the viewing public. The Angora and other longhaired breeds steadily lost popularity until they eventually vanished from the cat fancy.

Drolling the Elder (c1798). Again a white cat is the chosen subject. In the years that followed, Turkish and Persian cats became quite commonplace in portraits, especially those of children.

BIRTH OF THE CAT FANCY
The 19th century was in many ways the most interesting of all centuries from the perspective of cat owners. There was an insatiable appetite for curiosities, and many clubs and societies were formed. Cats had by now attained a considerable following. However, in the early years of the cat fancy this following was to be found mainly among the royalty, the landed gentry, and the upper levels of society. It was only these people who could afford desirable felines of the day. Of these desirable felines, there is little doubt the Turkish and Persians reigned supreme.

Even in the 19th century, the Turkish and Persian types were not always referred to as such. Many were simply called French or Eastern cats. Whether or not a given cat was Turkish or Persian may well have depended on which of these its owner wanted it to be! However, as cat shows

Opposite page: During the 19th century, the cat fancy blossomed and longhaired cats became THE cat to own. Still today it is the Persian's beautiful coat that makes it such a popular choice.

Exotic Shorthair

PERSIAN INFLUENCE
In 1901 the Blue Persian Cat Society was formed. It is the oldest longhair cat club in the world. With the passing years the Persian has been used to create new cat breeds, such as the Exotic Shorthair. It has also been used to introduce new colours and patterns into numerous breeds. Its popularity as a show cat is such that, without it, the cat fancy would not have been quite so appealing.

developed, those regarded as cat experts began to develop their own notions of what each of these two types should look like. This would shape the future of both breed types.

In his *The Book of Cats* of 1868, Charles H Ross describes the Angora much as della Valle had described the Persian. One notable difference he does add is that they were delicate cats with gentle dispositions. He describes the Persian as having very long and silken hair, 'perhaps more so than the Angora.' The use of 'perhaps more so' indicates that the difference between these breed types was by no means as clear cut as is often thought. He then continues, 'it is however differently coloured, being of a fine uniform grey...' Colour would therefore seem to have been an important consideration in distinguishing between these two Eastern cats at that time.

During this time more and more cat shows were successfully organised in Britain. The same was true for America and throughout Europe. In 1887 the National Cat Club was formed in Britain. Two years later it issued official standards for longhaired cats. In 1893 the first stud book was issued. By now the Persian was gaining more and more

devotees as its type improved and its coat became fuller and longer than that of the Angora.

When the standards were issued, a clear distinction was made between the longhaired breeds. The Persian coat was required to be fine, silky and very soft. The Angora was required to have a woollier coat and a definite brush-like tail. Interestingly, there was a longhaired Russian cat in those days. Its coat was required to be even woollier than that of the Angora.

In spite of the supposed distinction between these two breeds, it is of note that in 1903 the famous author and judge Francis Simpson is on record as having said that the differences

The Persians of the early 20th century looked more like the present-day Maine Coon, shown here.

The Persians of today bear little resemblance to the Persians of one hundred years ago, especially as their faces shortened.

between these two breeds was so fine that, 'I must be pardoned if I ignore the class of cat commonly called Angora which seems gradually to have disappeared.'

THE MODERN ERA

The present-day Persian bears little resemblance to the originals seen at the turn of the 20th century. These would best be likened to the present-day Maine Coon or Norwegian Forest cats. The changes taking place were observed from the early years of the cat fancy. John Jennings, a noted author and judge of the early cat shows, was very concerned at that time that the faces of the Persian were getting shorter.

However, nothing succeeds like success and the Persian was on a roll that has only begun to slow down in the last few years.

Even though there are signs its popularity has finally passed its peak, it still remains the world's most popular breed of cat. Its annual registration numbers are still greater than those of all the other longhaired breeds put together. The key to the success of this amazing breed is quite simply glamour with a capital G. Its history has always been associated with royalty, wealth and the finer things in life. It is, indeed, a truly royal cat among our domestic feline companions.

The Norwegian Forest cat as it appears today.

A *Portrait of the*
PERSIAN CAT

Before giving a description of the Persian, a point of clarification should be made about the name of this breed in Britain. In the early years of the cat fancy, there were a number of longhaired breeds. One by one they disappeared, the last being the Angora. At that point the name Persian was dropped and replaced by the term Longhaired. This general term embraced all of the various colours. These became breeds in their own right—which also meant having their own standard of points. The same situation existed in America.

With the passing years, other longhaired breeds came into being, which made the term used by the Governing Council of the Cat Fancy (GCCF) of Britain rather misleading. In America the term was sensibly dropped during the 1960s. The Persian again became just another breed. The GCCF overcame the situation by calling all other longhaired cats semi-longhaired. These were divided into the various breeds.

In more recent years, the GCCF reintroduced the name Persian, but in a form that complicated the situation for the beginner. Now there is a Long

Hair section, which includes all the Persian Long Hairs (meaning the various colour/patterns) and the Exotic Shorthair. The various Long Hair breeds are still judged according to their own standards. For the purposes of this chapter, the Persian is regarded as a single breed and the colour patterns merely varieties of it.

The breed and colour descriptions are based on official standards without being those of any single registration body. They will serve most needs. Those planning to breed and/or exhibit should obtain the breed standard appropriate to the association(s) where they choose to register their stock. The wording of all official standards for a given breed, while similar, is never exactly the same.

PERSIAN DESCRIPTION
The general impression of the Persian is of a solid, heavy-looking cat with an abundance of coat. Its facial expression should

Opposite page: The Colourpoint, known in America as the Himalayan, is a very popular colour variety of the Persian.

SEVEN DOZEN CHOICES!

Saying that the Persian is a 'colourful' breed would be quite the understatement. In Britain, there are 84 colours and patterns from which the cat owner can choose. In America, there are over 100! In Britain, each colour is considered a separate breed and many breeders specialise in certain colours or patterns, such as Smokes or Tortoiseshells.

impart its gentle nature. More so than in any other breed, the face of the Persian is very variable. It can range from the more traditional type to that which is extremely flat. These are called Ultra-Persians in Britain and Peke-faced in America.

Head: Massive, round and broad. Set on a thick short neck. The forehead is rounded, the cheeks full. The muzzle should be full, the jaws broad and strong.

Nose: This should be short and broad, in some varieties a 'snub' is required. A 'stop' should be evident, this meaning a clear break or indentation between the eyes where the forehead meets the nose.

The standard list of the GCCF states that an exaggeration of the nasal depression (the stop) may create breathing difficulties. This is often accompanied with blocked tear ducts. The nose is 'not to be excessively short.' The GCCF has in recent years introduced a 'nose' rule. This stipulates that the top of the nose leather must not be higher than the lower lid of the eye.

Eyes: Bold without bulging, they should be set far apart and of a brilliant colour.

Ears: Small and rounded at their tips. Not unduly open at their base, they should be set well apart and fit neatly into the contours of the head. Full ear furnishings, hairs that protrude from inside the ear, should be present.

Body: Medium to large in size, it should be cobby in its type. This means powerful, substantial and low to the ground. The chest should be deep and wide, the shoulders and rump massive.

Legs: Short and thick. They should be straight. The paws are round

In Britain the flat-faced Persians are referred to as Ultra-Persians, while in America they are called Peke-faced because of their similarity to the Pekingese dog's face.

and firm, preferably with hair tufts present. There are five toes on the front feet, four on the rear.

Tail: Short but not unduly so. Bushy.

Coat: Long and thick, fine in texture. It should be soft without being unduly woolly. A full fringe should cover the shoulder and extend to the chest between the front legs. During the summer months, the hair will be less dense, referred to as being 'out of coat.'

Teeth: Though not specifically referred to in all standards, teeth

DID YOU KNOW?
Almost all Tortoiseshells are female cats because this coat pattern, which includes patches of cream to red with black, is sex-linked. Male Torties are extremely rare and are incapable of reproducing.

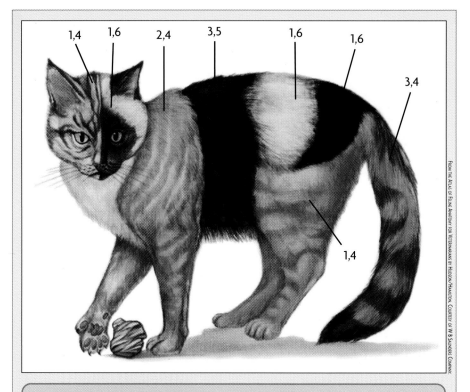

FROM THE ATLAS OF FELINE ANATOMY FOR VETERINARIANS BY HUDSON/HAMILTON. COURTESY OF W B SAUNDERS COMPANY.

PARTICOLOURED CAT

Not a new breed of feline, this 'particoloured cat' illustrates the many possibilities of the feline coat. Since cats come in three basic hair lengths, short, long and rex (curly), all three coat lengths are illustrated here. Additionally, different coat patterns, such as mackerel tabby, Abyssinian and self-coloured are depicted to demonstrate the differences.

1—3 COAT TYPES
1 Shorthair coat
2 Rex (curly) coat
3 Longhair coat

4—6 COAT COLOUR PATTERNS
4 Mackerel (tabby)
5 Abyssinian
6 Self-coloured

are often included in the list of withholding faults (disqualifying faults in America) applicable to all breeds. Ideally the teeth should display a level bite in any cat breed. But in the Persian, with its foreshortened jaw, this may not be the case. The standard list of the GCCF requires that the jaw should 'not be noticeably overshot or undershot.'

SKIN AND HAIRCOAT OF CATS

Schematic illustration of histologic layers of the integument skin.

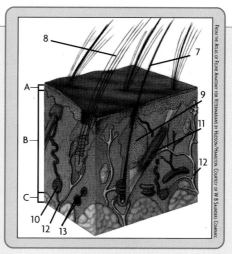

A Epidermis
B Dermis
C Subcutis

7 Primary hair
8 Secondary hairs
9 Area of sebaceous gland
10 Apocrine sweat gland
11 M. arrector pili
12 Nerve fibre
13 Cutaneous vessels
14 Tactile hair
15 Fibrous capsule
16 Venous sinus
17 Sensory nerve fibres
18 External root sheath
19 Hair papilla

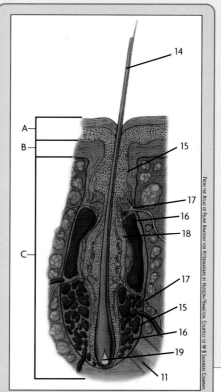

Schematic illustration of a tactile hair (whisker).

MEETING THE GRADE

Each breed of cat is judged by its breed standard, a written description of the ideal cat. A standard describes every aspect of the cat, from the tip of its nose to the tip of its tail, including all acceptable colours and personality. Breeders and judges use the breed standard to determine which cats are worthy of winning the ribbons and producing the kittens. Cats that fail to meet the grade should not be used in breeding programmes. These standards are approved by the governing cat organisation in each country.

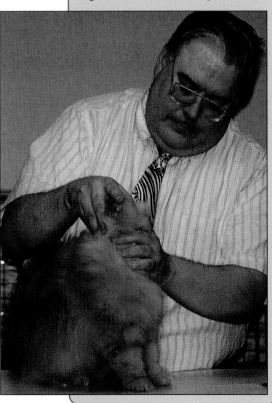

COLOURS AND PATTERNS

The Persian is available in a range of colours and patterns that will suit every possible taste. Some of these have been in the breed as far back as the first cat show, indeed since the breed has existed. Others have been added steadily over the years. Some are highly popular, others more rare. The following are all the colours and patterns currently recognised in this breed. They are divided into convenient groups.

SELF COLOURS

These colours are uniformly the same over the cat's entire body. In reality, this can be extremely difficult to achieve.

BICOLOURS

A bicolour is any colour and white. This pattern goes as far back as the earliest Persians. It was then called magpie or pied. For many years it was regarded as being of no value. However, with a revised standard allowing more flexibility in respect to the amount of white in the coat, the pattern now enjoys a growing following. This is no more than it deserves. A good bicolour is a most impressive Persian. The minimum white that should appear is on all four legs, the underbelly and chest. Colour may also appear in these areas. The face must show both a colour and white.

SELF COLOURS

COLOUR	DESCRIPTION	EYE COLOUR
BLACK	Lustrous dense black. Kittens may have white or grey hairs that should disappear as they mature. Excessive sunlight can give a brown hue to the coat.	**COPPER/DEEP ORANGE**
WHITE	Associated with uni- or bilateral deafness.	**BLUE, ORANGE OR ODD-EYED** (one eye of each colour)
BLUE	Considered to be 'the' classic Persian colour. Medium to pale blue. Grey is perhaps a better description. It is the dilution of black.	**COPPER/DEEP ORANGE**
CHOCOLATE	A warm medium to dark chocolate. This colour was introduced from the Siamese.	**COPPER/DEEP ORANGE**
LILAC	A warm lilac. A dove-grey colour with a pinkish hue. The dilution of chocolate.	**COPPER/DEEP ORANGE**
RED	A deep rich red. It is the only sex-linked colour in cats.	**COPPER/DEEP ORANGE**
CREAM	Medium to pale or buff cream. The dilution of red.	**COPPER/DEEP ORANGE**

Minimally, colour must be present on the head and the tail must be full colour, though some white is accepted. The eye colour is copper or deep orange. The following are the present bicolours, each of which will be combined with white: **black, blue, chocolate, lilac, red, cream, brown tabby, blue tabby, chocolate tabby, lilac tabby, red tabby and cream tabby.**

'WHEN IS A PERSIAN NOT A PERSIAN?'

When the Governing Council of the Cat Fancy (GCCF) decided to change the breed name from Persian to Long Hair, a most perplexing situation resulted. Since the term 'Long Hair' could describe any number of cat breeds, from the Maine Coon to the Birman, cat owners were not certain about what was a longhaired cat and what was a Long Hair. Fortunately the name Persian was reinstated and includes all of the different colour varieties, which rightly are considered separate varieties (or breeds).

EYE COLOUR

Eye colours in cats are determined based on the amounts of brown-black and yellow-red pigments in the eye. The rainbow of eye colours spans blue, green and copper, including all the various shades of these three colours. Many cats have eyes that appear blue and/or green, though there are no such pigments in the feline eye. These colours appear as 'optical illusions' known as the Tyndall Phenomenon that involves light waves. To create blue eyes, the dark pigment in the eyes absorbs the light rays and the effect is blue. Green eyes are created by light passing through yellow pigment, allowing blue rays to be reflected, the combination of colours creates the illusion of green.

Copper eyes in cats are more straightforward and are created by brown pigments modified by yellow or black, thus creating hazel, copper, orange and various shades of these darker colours.

TORTOISESHELL

The **tortoiseshell**, also known as particolour or tricolour, is a pattern in which a basically black cat has areas of red of various shades throughout the coat, including the extremities—face, tail and feet. The tortoiseshell is a sex-linked pattern. This means that male torties are exceedingly rare and invariably sterile. This is not an especially popular pattern in its full colour form, but in its diluted form of **blue-cream** it enjoys much more support. There is also a **chocolate tortie** and its diluted form, the **lilac**. Eye colour is copper/deep orange.

TORTOISESHELL & WHITE

The addition of white areas to the tortoiseshell immediately transforms the pattern into a very appealing and popular form. In the past it was called 'chintz.' It is called calico in America. The

The tortoiseshell is a tricoloured cat. The three-colour pattern is usually sex-linked and sex-limited. With rare exceptions, only females are tortoiseshells.

amount and placement of white in this variety are as for the bicolour. The colours available are **tortoiseshell** (tortie), **blue tortie, chocolate tortie** and **lilac tortie**. In each case, white is present.

TABBY

A very old pattern, the tabby in the Persian is no longer as popular as it was in the early years of the fancy. There are two types—mackerel and classic. In Britain the GCCF standardises only the classic in the Persian. In America both types have standards. In shorthaired breeds the tabby pattern is most striking, but far less so in any longhaired breed.

On the head, there should be a distinct letter 'M.' Down the spine there is a central dark unbroken

TABBY COLOURS

COLOUR	DESCRIPTION	EYE COLOUR
BROWN	Tawny sable ground with dense black markings.	ORANGE/COPPER
BLUE	Pale blue ground with darker blue markings.	ORANGE/COPPER
CHOCOLATE	Bronze ground with chocolate brown markings.	HAZEL OR COPPER
LILAC	Beige ground with lilac markings.	HAZEL OR COPPER
RED	Red ground with deeper rich red markings.	ORANGE/COPPER
SILVER	Silver ground with dense black markings.	GREEN OR HAZEL

line. On either side of this, another line is seen. On each flank, there is an oyster-shaped blotch. One or more unbroken rings surround this. On the shoulders, and viewed from above, the pattern takes the shape of butterfly wings. The legs should be barred with bracelets, the tail with rings. The chest and neck should carry unbroken necklaces, the more the better. The underbelly should carry spots. Markings on each side of the body and legs should be as identical as possible. Breeding quality tabbies is very difficult.

TORTIE TABBIES (TORBIE)

These are tabbies that are overlaid with red or cream. Both parts—tortie and tabby—must be clearly visible. The available colours, with the tabby colour given first, are: **brown/red, blue/cream, chocolate/red,** and **lilac/cream**. In each variety the eye colour is orange/copper.

The tortie tabby pattern can also be combined with white to create the **tortie tabby & white**. This is available in the same colours as the tortie tabby. The acceptable range of white and colour in the coat is the same as the bicolour: white appearing on all four legs, the underbelly and chest; face showing both a colour and white; and tail being full colour. Yet another combination pattern with the tabby is the **bicolour tabby &**

BEAUTY 'NOSE' NO GAIN

The steady reduction in nose length in the Persian on both sides of the Atlantic has gone hand in hand with a steady reduction (30–35%) in registration numbers over the last decade. Beauty is, of course, a very subjective quality, but evidence indicates that excessive exaggeration of features always comes at a price. That price is a steady loss of popularity. The decline in Persian registrations is in contrast with the increasing numbers of the Maine Coon and Birman. The implication is clear for those looking towards the future.

white. In this there must be no white hairs in the tabby or coloured hairs or shading in the white. Once again, the amount of white or tabby in the coat is the same as in the bicolour and white. Eye colour is orange / copper. Available colours are **black, blue, chocolate, lilac, red** and **cream**.

TIPPED COAT PATTERNS

For many people, the numerous tipped coat patterns are seen at their best in the longhaired breeds, and especially so in the Persian. There are three levels of tipping.

SMOKE

This is a pattern of contrasts. The undercoat is as near to white as possible. This quickly starts to shade to a colour, which then continues to the tip of the hair.

When at rest the colour appears to be uniform, but once on the move the hair parts and reveals the underlying white undercoat. The flanks and sides of the body shade to silver; the mask and feet are coloured. The frill and ear tufts are silver. Eye colour is always orange/copper.

SHADED COLOURS

COLOUR	DESCRIPTION	EYE COLOUR
SILVER	White with black tipping.	EMERALD OR BLUE-GREEN
GOLDEN	Apricot undercoat becoming golden at the tip.	EMERALD OR BLUE-GREEN
RED-SHADED CAMEO	White evenly shaded with red.	ORANGE/COPPER
CREAM-SHADED CAMEO	White evenly shaded with cream.	ORANGE/COPPER
PEWTER	Similar to silver but a little darker.	ORANGE/COPPER

The Colourpoint is a result of crossing the Persian with the Siamese many years ago.

The following are the present colours: **black, blue, chocolate, lilac, red, tortie** (the tipping is black, red and cream, broken into patches), **cream** (the body is cream shading to white, the mask and feet cream, the frill and ear tufts white), **blue-cream** (tipping a mixture of blue and cream intermingled), **chocolate tortie** and **lilac tortie.**

SHADED

In this pattern the tipping extends up to one-third of the hair, thus not as far down the shaft as in the smoke.

LIGHT TIPPING

Under this heading there are some most attractive varieties. In each case the hairs are only coloured at their very tips, so they are lighter than the shaded varieties. The **chinchilla** is white, tipped with black to give a silvery white appearance. The chin, ear furnishings, stomach and chest are white. Eye colour is emerald or blue-green. The **red shell cameo** (sometimes called red chinchilla) has a silvery appearance delicately dusted with pink. In the **cream shell cameo** the pink is replaced with cream. Eye colour is

COLOURPOINT

SOLID POINT COLOURS

POINT COLOUR	BODY COLOUR
SEAL BROWN	Beige shading to creamy white.
BLUE	Bluish white shading to white.
CHOCOLATE	Ivory shading to white.
LILAC	Magnolia white shading to white.
RED	Apricot shading to white.
CREAM	Lighter cream shading to white.

TORTIE POINT COLOURS

POINT COLOUR	BODY COLOUR
SEAL BROKEN WITH SHADES OF RED	Toning creamy body colour.
BLUE-CREAM BLUE BROKEN WITH SHADES OF CREAM	Glacial to creamy white.
CHOCOLATE BROKEN WITH SHADES OF RED	Ivory to apricot white.
LILAC-CREAM LILAC BROKEN WITH SHADES OF CREAM	Magnolia to creamy.

TABBY POINT COLOURS

Tabby is restricted to the points. The colours are seal, blue, chocolate, lilac, red and cream.

TORTIE TABBY POINT COLOURS

Both the tortie and the tabby elements must be present though the extent and distribution of these are not important. The colours are seal, blue-cream, chocolate and lilac-cream.

With a Colourpoint, the colour is restricted to the points of the cat: mask, ears, legs, feet and tail.

orange/copper. The final two varieties of tipped hair types are the **tortoiseshell cameo** and the **blue-cream cameo**. In these the intensity of tipping can vary.

COLOURPOINT

The colourpoint is a very popular colour pattern. In America it is known as the Himalayan (after the rabbit of that pattern). It is the result of crossing the Persian with the Siamese. This was done many years ago and in numerous countries. The Himalayan of America was established experimentally as long ago as 1936. The pattern gained its first official status in Britain as the Colourpoint Longhair during 1955. This followed eight years of

planned breeding by Mr B Stirling Webb, a Siamese breeder. Examples were exported to America and the breed gained its official status there in 1957.

Although originally a hybrid, any genetic relationship to the Siamese has long since vanished— other than in the colour pattern. As suggested by its British name, the colour is restricted to the points of the cat. This means the mask, ears, legs, feet and tail. The mask should cover the entire face. Males tend to develop more extensive masks than females. There should be a good contrast between the point's colour and the rest of the body. Clearly, this will be less striking in the paler colours.

This Persian is too heavy.

The Ultra-Persian, so called because of its flattened face.

This Persian has the preferred body outline
indicating its weight is normal.

The preferred face of the Persian.

Correct ears.

Bad ears; too high.

Bad ears; too large and pointed.

The eyes are too small and too close together.

The preferred eye size and shape.

This pattern is thermo-sensitive. This means that in high ambient temperatures the colour tends to lighten. In cooler temperatures it darkens. However, there are limits to the extent of this variation. As the cat gets older, its circulation to the bodily extremities is not so good. The result is that the colour gets darker. Kittens are born without colour points, these starting to show themselves after a few weeks. In all varieties, the eyes should be a pure vivid blue.

In Britain, the potential Persian owner can choose from 84 colour pattern combinations. Other colours in various patterns not presently standardised are exhibited as Any Other Colour (AOC). In America,

COAT PATTERNS

Agouti	Pigments band the hair, named after the rodent that possesses this pattern.
Non-agouti	Coat colour exhibits a self colour or carries two or more colours.
Shell	Darker colour on tips of the hair; lower portion lighter in colour.
Shaded	Darker colour extends further than the tip, as in the shell.
Bicolour	Solid colour with white pattern.

where both the mackerel and the van patterns are standardised, the range exceeds 100.

A lovely black-and-white Bicolour Persian Cat. For a Bicolour, the face must display both a colour and white.

A dilute calico Persian Cat. Calico (tortoiseshell and white) is a female-only variety.

Purchasing a PERSIAN CAT

THE PURCHASING PROCESS

Never rush into the purchase of a companion who is to be given the freedom of your home and will become an integral part of your life. A Persian may live 20 or more years. This is a long time. It is very prudent to take all those steps that will minimise the chances of your ever regretting the choice you make. Once you have decided on the sex, age, reason for purchase (pet, show or breeding) and desired colour pattern, proceed cautiously, heeding all the advice given here. By following a planned process of selection, you will also gain much useful information.

Given its glamorous looks, it is no wonder the Persian is so popular. Before the decision to purchase is made, however, careful consideration should be given to the implications and responsibilities of cat ownership. If more owners would do this, there would be far fewer half-starved pets roaming our streets or having to live in local animal rescue centres.

OWNER RESPONSIBILITY

The initial cost of a Persian represents only a fraction of its lifetime's cost. The first question is, 'Can you afford one?' The kitten needs vaccinations to protect it against various diseases. Boosters are then required every year. Cat food is more costly than that for dogs. There is also the cost of cat litter every week. Periodic vet checks and treatment for illness or accident must be allowed for. When holidays are taken, you may need to board the pet at a cattery.

From the outset there will be additional costs apart from that of the kitten. It will need a basket, carrying box, feeding and grooming utensils, scratching post and maybe a collar and a few toys.

If you have any doubts at all about being able to supply all these needs, it is best not to obtain a cat.

Other matters also need careful thought. If you are planning to have a family, will your love for the Persian be maintained once a baby arrives? Cats are generally not a problem with family newcomers providing they are not ignored or treated as being a threat to the baby. Never purchase a kitten for a child unless you want one yourself. If you are elderly, it is only fair to consider what would happen to your cherished pet if it were to outlive you or if you were to become hospitalised for long periods.

It is most unfortunate that many people rush into the purchase of cats on an impulse. They then find they cannot cope if problems, and extra costs, ensue. Some lose interest in the pet once it matures past its kitten stage. The evidence of these realities is easily seen in the growing number of cats abandoned or taken to animal shelters every year. Invariably their owners will make feeble excuses for why the cat cannot be kept. In truth, they did not stop to consider at the outset what responsible ownership entailed.

Finally, the Persian is a very demanding breed. It is not a cat that will suit those people who do not have time to devote to it, and more especially to its grooming

DOCUMENTATION

When you take delivery of your kitten, certain paperwork should come with it:

1. Three-to-five-generation pedigree.
2. Breeder signed registration application form or change of owner registration form. This assumes the breeder has registered stock. If he has not, the kitten cannot be registered at a later date. It is worth less than the kitten with registration paperwork. You are not recommended to purchase a kitten from unregistered parents.
3. Certificates of health, vaccination and neutering, if this has been effected. Ideally, it is desirable that the kitten's parents have been tested negative for major diseases. Additionally, the breeder should know the blood group of your kitten. This may be of importance at a later date.
4. Details of worming or other treatments attended.
5. Diet sheet, feeding timetable and brand names of food items used. This diet should be maintained for at least ten days while the kitten adjusts to the trauma of moving home.
6. Signed receipt for monies paid.
7. Signed copy of any guarantees. Not all breeders give a guarantee on the reasonable grounds that once the kitten leaves their care its onward well-being is no longer under their control.

TAKING KITTY HOME

Arrange collection of the kitten as early in the day as possible. If a long journey is involved, be sure to take a few breaks so kitty does not become carsick. Do not make stops to show the kitten to friends; this represents a health hazard. Once home, offer the kitten a drink, then allow it to sleep if it so requires. Children must be educated to handle a kitten gently, never to tease it, and to respect its sleeping privacy. Until it is litter trained, it should be restricted to the kitchen or another room with an easy-to-clean floor surface.

intestinal hairballs that could prove very dangerous to the pet's health.

It must also be said that while a Persian will usually fit into any family unit, it is best in small families where the house is not overrun with young children and other pets who live a hectic lifestyle. The Persian is a refined cat that prefers a quiet and leisurely existence. For those living alone or couples who may be away from the home for a number of hours each day, the purchase of two kittens is a good idea, as they would provide company for each other.

KITTEN OR ADULT?

Most potential owners normally want a kitten because it is so cute, cuddly and playful. A kitten is easily trained and has not yet developed bad habits, which the older Persian may have done. This said, if you plan to breed or exhibit there are advantages in obtaining a young adult. Other potential owners, such as the elderly, may benefit by avoiding the demanding needs of a young kitten. In both these instances, a good age is when the youngster is

needs. It cannot be over-stressed that a Persian needs grooming every single day. If not, its beautiful coat will rapidly deteriorate into a mass of tangles and mats. This will prompt the cat to vigorously self-groom. Any loose hairs that would have been brushed out of the coat may be swallowed. These could result in

Opposite page: All longhaired cats require daily brushing. If you are unable or unwilling to give a Persian the grooming care it requires, you should select a shorthaired cat.

Opposite page: There are differences between the behaviour of toms and queens. So sex matters when making a choice. However, your choice of coloration is strictly personal and has no bearing on a cat's personality.

9–15 months old. Even a fully mature Persian may prove an excellent choice for some owners.

Kittens should not be obtained under 12 weeks old, though 14–16 is better. No reputable breeder will sell them younger than this. Less caring breeders will let them go to new homes as young as eight weeks of age. Such juveniles will barely have been weaned. They will not have developed the needed resistance to major diseases. They are more likely to become stressed by the premature removal from their mother and siblings. Their vaccinations will not be fully effective. These facts will dramatically increase the risk of immediate problems.

SEX & COLOUR PATTERN

If it is to be purely a pet, the Persian's gender is unimportant. Both are delightful. Males are usually larger, bolder and more outgoing. Females tend to be more discerning about which humans they like. However, each Persian is an individual. Its character and health, more than its sex, should be the basis of selection. Again, the sex is unimportant for the potential exhibitor. It is not even necessary for the cat to be sexually 'entire.' Classes for neuters are featured in shows.

Those with breeding aspirations are advised to obtain only females. All pet owners should regard neutering (males) and spaying (females) as obligatory. Today this can be effected at any age after eight weeks.

The colour pattern is a matter of personal preference. It should never be placed ahead of health and character. Some colours and patterns will be more readily available than others will. The more popular varieties may be less costly than the rarer ones. This would generally not apply to prospective breeding or exhibition individuals where type quality will be as important as colour or pattern.

LOOK BEFORE YOU LEAP

It is important you view as many Persian kittens as you can. This gives you a good mental picture of what a healthy typical example should look like and cost for the quality and colour you want. Normally, you will get what you pay for. If you look for the cheapest kitten, there will be a sound reason why it is the cheapest!

The best place to start your search is a cat show. At these most of the colour varieties will be on display. Purchase the show catalogue. It lists all the exhibitors and their addresses. You can see if any live in your immediate locality. Whenever possible it is best to purchase locally so you can visit the home of the breeder. Some will insist you do so in

HOMEMADE TOYS

Cats love to play and pet shops have a lot of cat toys to choose from. Sometimes, however, people give their cats homemade toys. These can be harmful to your cat, as they could have pieces that could break off and be swallowed. Only give your pet toys from a pet shop that have been proven safe for cats.

order to be satisfied that you will make a good owner.

Shows and breeders are advertised in the various cat magazines available from newsagents. You can also contact a major cat registry. They will supply a list of national and regional clubs, which are usually able to supply breeder lists. When visiting a breeder, always make an appointment. Try to visit no more than one a day. This reduces the risk you may transport pathogens (disease-causing organisms) from one establishment to the next. Selecting a good breeder is a case of noting the environment in which the cats are kept, the attitude of the owner to you and their cats, and how friendly and healthy the kittens look. It is vital the chosen kitty has an outgoing personality. It must not appear timid or very shy. This indicates a lack of breeder socialisation or a genetic weakness in its temperament. Either way, it is not a kitten you should select.

CAT LITTER

The litter that is used in cat boxes can be very variable and in many cases cats reject the use of a cat box because of the litter. Certainly if your cat rejects the use of the cat box, you should try different litters. You can start with the litters available at your local pet shop, then you can try sand, dirt, old rags, cedar shavings or whatever will appeal to your cat. Several cat owners grow clover in a tray and their cats seem to prefer that. However, the tray is kept outdoors and the cats may simply be marking the clover tray rather than using it for elimination purposes.

The selection of a Persian depends upon your needs. If you want to show your cat, then you should find a prize-winning breeder and discuss your ambitions. If you haven't too much time to spend with your Persian, consider buying two of them so they can keep each other company.

CHOOSING A KITTEN

If you choose the breeder wisely, and especially if a friend recommends him, this will remove all problems related to your making a poor choice. However, a little knowledge on what to look for will not go amiss. Observe the kittens from a distance to ensure none is unduly lethargic, which is never a good sign. If any display signs of illness, this should bring to an end any further thoughts of purchase from that source. A reputable breeder would not allow an ill kitten to remain within its litter.

It is always advisable to select a kitten that shows particular interest in you. Persians are very discerning. If both of you are drawn to each other, this will greatly enhance the bonding essential for a strong relationship.

Once a particular kitten has been selected, it should be given a close physical inspection. The eyes and nose must show no signs of weeping or discharge. The ears will be erect and fresh smelling. The coat should look healthy, never dry and dull. There must be no signs of parasites in the fur. There will be no bald areas of fur, nor bodily swellings or abrasions. Lift the tail and inspect the anal region. This must be clean with no indication of congealed faecal matter. Any staining of the fur indicates current or recent diarrhoea.

A HEALTHY KITTEN

Closely inspect any kitten before making a final decision. Keep in mind the following points:

Eyes and Nose: Clean and clear with no signs of discharge.

Ears: Fresh smelling and erect.

Coat: Healthy, not dull or dry.

Anal region: Clean with no staining of the fur.

Feet: Four toes on each foot, plus a dewclaw on the inside of each front leg.

Teeth: Correct bite.

There should be no signs of parasites or bald areas of fur. A potbelly may indicate worms.

Your local pet shop will have scratching posts in various sizes and prices.

The kitten must not display a potbelly. This may indicate worms or other internal disorders. Check the teeth to be sure of a correct bite. Bear in mind that the jawbones do not develop at the same rate. Minor imperfections may correct themselves (they may also get worse) but major faults will not. Inspect the feet to see there are four toes on each, plus a dewclaw on the inside of each front leg.

With respect to the colour, there is no link between this and health other than deafness in certain white varieties. Any faults in the colour or its placement will only be of importance in breeding or exhibition individuals. The potential breeder/exhibitor should obtain a copy of the official standard so they are *au fait* with all colour, pattern and bodily faults of the breed.

KITTY SHOPPING SPREE

Certain accessories should be regarded as obligatory and obtained before the kitten arrives in your home.

SCRATCHING POST

This will save the furniture from being abused! There are many models, some being simple posts, others are combined with play stations and sleeping quarters. These are the best.

While there are many amateur scratching posts available, you should only buy a scratching post made by professionals because some of the carpets used may be defective and injurious to your Persian.

Your local pet shop can show you the most suitable litterbox for your cat.

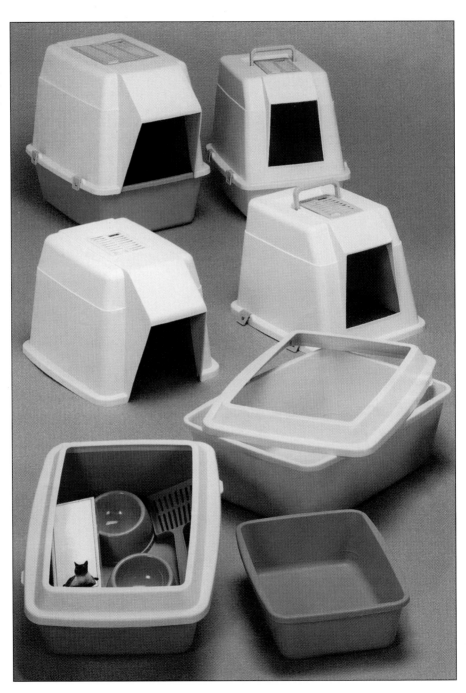

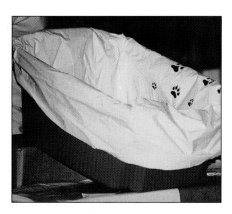

LITTERBOX
Some are open trays; others are domed to provide extra privacy. Yet others have special bases in which odour removers are fitted.

CAT LITTER
There are numerous types on the market, each offering advantages and drawbacks. Avoid the low-cost types that contain a lot of dangerous dust. Use those that are fully biodegradable.

FOOD/WATER DISHES
Polished metal has the longest wear life. Earthenware is less costly than metal and superior to the plastic types.

ADOPTING AN ADULT
Some owners, such as the elderly, may benefit by adopting an adult Persian. They can avoid the demanding needs of a young kitten and enjoy the advantages of a well-trained adult, making grooming an easier task. Breeders and exhibitors can also benefit from purchasing an older cat because it is easier to assess the quality. Sometimes, though, older cats can have bad habits that are hard to break. So if you are thinking about obtaining an older Persian, it is important to thoroughly investigate possible behavioural and health problems.

Litterbox liners are available to make cleaning your cat's litterbox an easy task.

Purchase the best quality that you can afford when purchasing items for your Persian.

Your local pet shop will have a variety of cat toys with which you can entertain yourself and your cat.

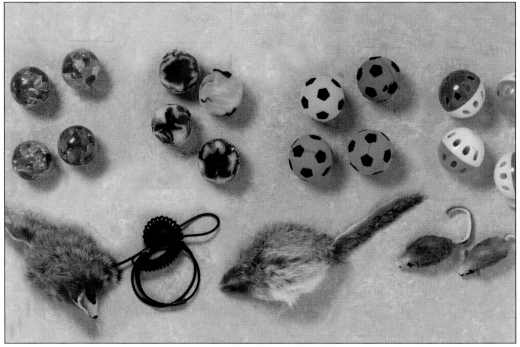

Daily grooming of your Persian with a good-quality brush is important.

GROOMING TOOLS

These will comprise a good-quality bristle brush, a fine-toothed comb, nail trimmers and a soft chamois leather.

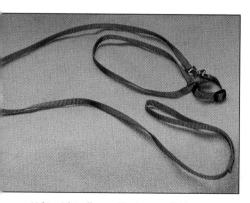

Lightweight collars and leads are available at your local pet shop.

CAT COLLAR AND/OR HARNESS

Select elasticised collars. Be sure a name and address disc or barrel is fitted to this. A harness must be a snug but comfortable fit if it is to be effective.

CAT CARRYING BOX

Essential for transporting the cat to the vet or other places, as well as for home restriction when needed. Be sure it is large enough to accommodate a fully-grown Persian, not just a kitten. The choice is between collapsible models, soft plastic types and, the best choice, those made of wood or fibreglass.

A cat carrying box is an absolute necessity for transporting your pet to the vet. It is also needed if you intend to travel with your Persian.

Providing a Safe Home for Your
PERSIAN CAT

For a kitten its human environment holds many dangers. Its owner must protect it from these until it becomes agile and wiser. The following dangers lurk in typical households. Always check whether there are additional ones in your home. The most important decision you need to make from the outset is whether or not the kitten is to be given outdoor liberty.

HOW MUCH FREEDOM?

More than at any time in the past the question of how much freedom a cat should be given is the subject of heated debate. It is a very subjective matter. Here the more pertinent points are given so you can relate these to your home location. These, to a very large degree, should influence your decision.

Cats living in or close to an urban area are at the highest safety risk. The amount of traffic is such that death from road accidents is a major concern. In such environments there are large populations of dogs, some of which are feral. Injury or death from dog attacks is therefore another major source of danger to a feline.

Urban cat populations are also extremely high. Far too many cats are living a virtually feral existence. These are tough, street-wise cats that often carry fleas and other parasites that are vectors of disease. Some will be carriers of, or infected with, feline leukaemia and other deadly diseases.

THE GARAGE AND SHED

These two buildings are very dangerous for a kitten. Sharp and heavy tools, nails, glass jars, garden weed killers, and open tins of paint are but a sampling of the items the average family uses or stores in these. A kitten may clamber into the engine compartment of a vehicle. This could be fatal if the owner happened to start the engine before the kitten had removed itself. Always know where the kitten is.

The typical feline family pet can be badly injured if it becomes engaged in fights with these roaming bullies. Furthermore, their very presence in and around a gentle cat's garden can cause the pet severe stress. This can make it fearful of stepping outside its home. In some instances it may cause the pet to actually leave its home.

Sadly, as if these risks were not enough, there are also too many people who will steal a pedigree cat, the more so if it is friendly. Add to this the number of abusive people who do not like cats' venturing into their gardens, and the scenario is not good. Finally, free-roaming cats also take a heavy toll on local bird and wildlife populations.

Taking these various facts into account, the urban cat is best kept indoors. It can enjoy the benefit of the outdoors if supplied with a roomy aviary-type exercise pen. Some cats can be trained to walk on a lead. This allows outdoor enjoyment, even if this is restricted to the garden. When walking your cat in public places, use only a harness. This is much safer than a collar.

In contrast to urban situations, the cat living in a rural environment is far safer, the more so if there are no immediate neighbours or busy roads. Even so, it is wise to restrict the cat's outdoor freedom to daylight

BE ONE JUMP AHEAD
Seemingly innocuous things, such as doors, can become life-threatening should they suddenly slam shut on a kitten due to a through draught. When windows and external doors are open, be sure internal doors are secured with a doorstop. At all times be one jump ahead of a kitten in terms of identifying dangerous situations.

hours. During the night it is more likely to get run over or to threaten local wildlife.

Those living between the extremes of isolated areas and busy urban environments should consider the local risk factor. Generally it is best to keep the cat indoors but to provide an outdoor exercise pen.

HOUSEHOLD DANGERS
Within its home a kitten is best viewed as an accident waiting to happen! The most dangerous room is the kitchen. Hot electric hobs, naked flames from gas rings,

You must think of your local veterinary surgeon as your cat's second best friend. Choose your vet with care.

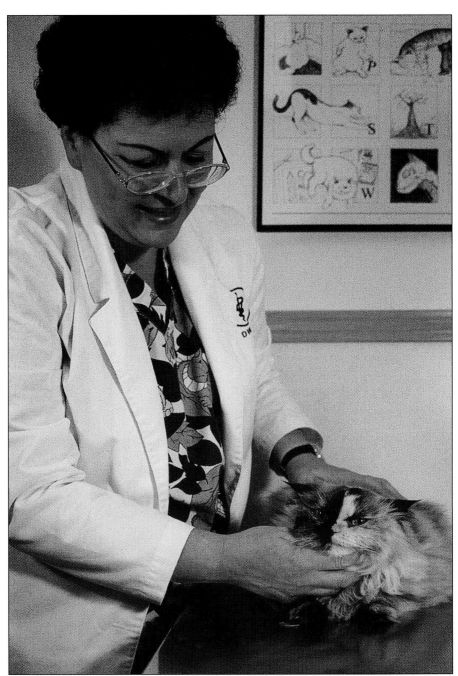

boiling pans of food or water, and sinks full of water are obvious hazards. An iron left on its board with cable trailing to the floor is an invitation to a kitten to jump up—with potentially fatal consequences. Washing machines or spin dryers with clothes in them, and their doors open, are inviting places to nap. Always check the kitty isn't inside if the door has been left open. Cupboards containing poisonous or other dangerous substances should always be kept securely closed.

In the living room the normal dangers are aquariums without hoods, unguarded fires, electric bar heaters, poisonous indoor plants, trailing electrical wires, and ornaments that may be knocked over by a mischievous kitty. Toilets can be fatal to an over-curious kitten. The same is true of a bath containing water. Balconies should be safeguarded to remove the potential for the kitten to slip and fall.

OTHER DANGERS

Other potential dangers are when electric tools are left lying about and connected to power outlets—even worse if they are left on, as with bench saws. If the kitten is given freedom to exercise in a garden containing a pond, the kitten must be under constant supervision. Cherished ornaments should be placed out of reach of the kitten, as much for their safety as to any danger they may present to the kitty. It's not always the direct danger of something that can be the problem. If an ornament or similar item crashes to the floor, this can startle the kitten into a panicked departure! The kitten could then fall from a shelf in its haste.

THE TRAVELLING CAT

Whenever your cat needs to be taken on a car journey, never let it travel loose in the vehicle, which is illegal. It must always be in its carrying box. If a cat were to go under the clutch or brake pedal when the car was moving, this would be dangerous to all occupants. A cat might also spring from one seat to another which might distract the driver. This could have disastrous results.

Never leave a cat more than a few minutes alone in a car on a hot day. The temperature can rise dramatically to the point the cat is unable to breathe. It could die of heatstroke. Always leave a window partially open, but not so much that the agile cat could escape.

Feeding Your
PERSIAN CAT

Today the feeding of cats has been reduced to its most simple level with the availability of many scientifically prepared commercial diets. However, this fact can result in owners becoming casual in their approach to the subject. While the main object of a given diet is to provide the ingredients that promote healthy growth and maximum immunity to disease, it also fulfils an important secondary role.

It must maintain in the cat a psychological feeling of well-being that avoids nutritionally related stress problems or syndromes. By ensuring the diet is balanced, of good variety, and never monotonous, these dual

roles will be achieved. This approach will also avoid the situation of the cat's becoming a finicky eater.

BALANCE AND VARIETY

A balanced diet means one that contains all of the major ingredients—protein, fats, carbohydrates, vitamins and minerals—in the ratios needed to ensure maximum growth and health. Variety means supplying foods in a range of forms that will maintain and stimulate the cat's interest in its meals. Commercially formulated foods come in three levels of moisture: low, semi-moist and moist (tinned foods).

Generally, the dried and moist forms are the most popular. Dried cat foods have the advantage they can be left in the cat dish for longer periods of time than tinned foods.

They are ideal for supplying on a free-choice basis. Like the tinned varieties, they come in a range of popular flavours.

In order to meet the specific needs of a kitten, there are specially formulated foods available. These contain higher protein levels needed by a growing kitten. As it grows, the

MILK AND CATS
Milk, although associated with cats, is not needed once kittenhood has passed. Indeed, excess milk can create skeletal and other problems. Some cats may become quite ill if given too much. They are unable to digest its lactose content. However, small amounts may be appreciated as a treat. Goat's milk, diluted condensed milk and low-lactose milks are better than cow's milk.

kitten can be slowly weaned onto the adult types. There are also special brands available from vets for any kitten or cat that may have a dietary problem as well as special diets for the older cat. These may need lower ratios of certain ingredients, such as proteins and sodium, so as to reduce the workload of the liver.

Flavours should be rotated so interest in meals is maintained. This also encourages familiarity with different tastes. Naturally, Persians will display a greater liking for certain flavours and brands than for others.

FRESH FOODS

To add greater variety and interest, there are many fresh foods that Persians enjoy. Some will be very helpful in cleaning the teeth and exercising jaw muscles. All have the benefit of providing different textures and smells that help stimulate the palate. Feed these foods two or three times a week as treats or occasionally as complete meals.

Cooked poultry, including the skin, but minus the bones, is usually a favourite, as is quality raw or cooked mincemeat. Cooked beef on the bone gives the cat something to enjoy. Cooked white fish, as well as tinned tuna or sardines, is an example of an ocean delight. Never feed raw fish; this can prove dangerous, even fatal. Although cats rarely

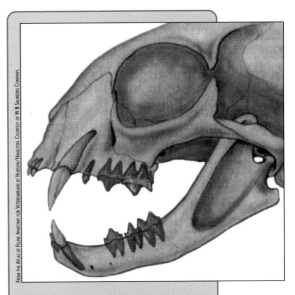

FROM THE ATLAS OF FELINE ANATOMY FOR VETERINARIANS BY HUDSON/HAMILTON. COURTESY OF W B SAUNDERS COMPANY.

MEET THE MEAT-EATERS

Since cats are carnivorous, their teeth are designed to bite and cut. Except for crunching dried foods, cats do very little chewing. They have the fewest teeth of any common domestic mammal—typically 30 (although there are some variations). The canines usually are more developed than the incisors.

enjoy items such as rice, pasta or cooked vegetables, these can nonetheless be finely chopped and mixed with meats or fish. Some Persians may develop a taste for them. Various cheeses and scrambled or boiled eggs will often be appreciated—but never give raw eggs.

If the diet is balanced and

varied, the addition of vitamin and mineral supplements is unnecessary and can actually prove dangerous. While certain of these compounds are released from the body if in excess, others are not. They are stored and can adversely affect efficient metabolism. If a cat shows loss of condition and disinterest in its food, discuss its diet with a vet.

The food dish should be placed in a quiet area. Certainly not near a door!

HOW MUCH TO FEED

Food intake is influenced by many factors. These are the cat's age, activity level, the ambient temperature (more is eaten in the colder months), the cat's breeding state (rearing kittens) and the quality of the food. Always follow the breeder's recommendations on diet until your kitten has settled into your home. Thereafter the needed quantity will increase as the kitten gets older, until full maturity at about two to three years of age.

The food needs of a queen with kittens may differ from the needs of a cat under normal circumstances. Check with your local veterinary surgeon.

As a basic guide, a four-month-old kitten will require four meals a day. At six months old, one meal can be dropped. By twelve months of age, only two meals will be required, possibly only one if dried foods are also available on a free-choice basis. As the number of meals is decreased, the quantity must be increased at the others.

FOOD AND WATER CONTAINERS

Persians are not too fussy over what vessels are used for supplying their food and water, but a few tips are useful. Persians do not like to eat from dirty dishes anymore than you would. Their food bowl should be washed after each meal. Water containers should be washed and replenished every day. Saucers make ideal food plates. Wide feeders from your pet shop are excellent for dried biscuits. Pot or polished metal containers are better buys than plastic. They last longer and are easier to keep clean.

Discuss how much to feed and what to feed with your veterinary surgeon or the breeder from whom you acquired the kitten.

IMPORTANT DON'TS

- Do not let your cat become a fussy eater. Cats are not born fussy but are made that way by their owners. Your cat will not starve if given the correct food, but it may try to convince you otherwise. However, a cat that refuses all foods offered may be ill. Contact your vet.
- Do not give a cat sweet and sticky foods. These provide no benefit and, if eaten, will negatively affect normal appetite for wholesome foods.
- Do not feed vitamin and mineral supplements to either kittens or adults unless under advice from a veterinary surgeon. Excess vitamins and minerals can be as bad for their health as a lack of them. They will create potentially dangerous cellular metabolic imbalances.
- Do not give any questionable foods, such as those that smell or look 'off.' If in doubt discard them. Always store foods in cool darkened cupboards. Be sure all foods from the freezer and refrigerator are fully thawed.

Opposite page: Having short muzzles, Persians sometimes have a problem feeding from deep dishes. Consider this when purchasing your food and water bowls.

Having a short muzzle, the Persian does not like to place its head into deep food dishes nor does it like its whiskers to touch the inner walls. Ensure dishes are wide and shallow.

WHERE AND WHEN TO FEED
Usually, the best place to feed a cat is in the kitchen. It is important to place food and water dishes as far away from the litter tray as possible. This could otherwise deter the cat from eating. Cats also like to eat in quiet comfort. Meals should be spread across the entire day. When the number is reduced to two, these should be given in the morning and evening at convenient times. For the Persian given outdoor freedom, it is best to feed the main meal in the evening. This encourages it to come home at this time. It can then be kept indoors overnight.

EATING LIKE CATS AND DOGS
You should never feed your cat dog food because dogs and cats have different dietary needs. Cats have a much higher need for fats than dogs, and kittens need more than adult cats. Cats also require unusually high levels of dietary protein as compared with those of dogs. The foods you choose for your cat must supply these essential components.

Grooming Your
PERSIAN CAT

The longhaired coat of the Persian is undoubtedly the essence of the breed. To neglect grooming this magnificent fur is sacrilege. If the coat is not attended on a daily basis, it will soon look bedraggled and cause considerable discomfort to the cat. Mats will form that will prevent dead hair from being shed. These will soon enough become entangled with other debris—grass, small sticks, cat litter and even food. It is, therefore, most important that a prospective Persian owner fully accepts that grooming is crucial with this breed. It should never be a chore. If done regularly, it will help bond the cat to its owner. The cat will always be a joy to behold and its owner will be very proud.

Regular grooming also enables close examination of the cat for any signs of problems. These include fleas or mites, small wounds, abrasions, swellings and bald areas. The grooming process should include inspection of the cat's ears, teeth and nails.

Always purchase the best-quality items. Avoid the use of low-cost plastic-toothed combs and brushes. These create static electricity. This results in flyaway and crinkled hair that is not the best state for this breed's coat.

Before we discuss grooming procedures, a few general points should be made. So that grooming

If your Persian became accustomed to being brushed when it was a kitten, it will enjoy the brushing after it matures. Simply put, you must brush your Persian on a daily basis.

is not reduced to a battle between cat and owner, it is essential the kitten finds this a pleasurable experience. This will not be the case if the owner is heavy-handed in his or her use of the brush, and more especially the comb. The tenderest parts of the cat are its underbody parts and tail. These must be groomed with this fact always in mind, doubly so if tags have formed.

Some owners groom the cat on their laps, others on tables. This author prefers a table. Ensure the surface is of a non-slip type— a rubber mat is recommended for this purpose. Again, some owners will commence with the comb, but it is better to use the brush first. It is more forgiving, thus gentle. It avoids unnecessary pulling of the hair.

BRUSHING

Commence on the neck and brush down the fur to the tail. This will remove any small bits of detritus in the coat. Next brush down the chest, body sides and flanks. With the kitten now familiar with the feel of the brush, gently turn and secure the kitty on its back while its belly is brushed. Groom the tail by forming a parting with the brush and grooming the fur at right angles.

This completed, brush against the lie of the fur. Commence on the neck and brush a few inches at a time, working around the

GROOMING EQUIPMENT

The following will be required for complete grooming:
1. Round-ended, cushioned pin brush
2. Bristle brush
3. Medium-toothed metal comb with handle
4. Flea comb
5. A pair of guillotine nail clippers
6. Baby powder (if the Persian is dark coloured and required for exhibition, a soft chamois leather is useful)
7. Supply of cotton wool and cotton buds
8. Plastic pouring jug
9. Spray attachment for taps
10. Cat shampoo (those for dogs are not suitable for felines. A baby shampoo can be used but is not as effective as one formulated for cats)
11. One or two quality towels
12. Good hair dryer (the quieter the better)
13. Non-slip rubber mat
14. Good-sized plastic bowl with a rubber mat placed inside (to use as bath if sink is not suitable)
15. Medium-soft toothbrush and feline toothpaste (a saline solution is an alternative, but less tasty)
16. An appropriately sized plastic or other container in which to keep kitty's boutique apparel

HAIRBALLS (Trichobezoar)

When cats self groom, they invariably swallow some of their hairs. Normally these do not create a problem. However, if many dead hairs are in the coat these may be licked and swallowed to accumulate in the stomach as hairballs. These are more common in longhaired breeds than in those with short hair. Hairballs may create intestinal blockages which may so irritate the cat's intestinal tract that it vomits the hairball or voids it via its faecal matter.

If the hairball is not removed, and the cat displays reduced appetite, veterinary assistance is needed. Regular grooming greatly reduces the risk of this condition. Additionally, a teaspoon of liquid paraffin or other laxative once a week may be helpful in cats prone to this problem, but it is unlikely to remove an existing hairball. Pineapple juice containing the enzyme bromelain may break down small furballs. One teaspoonful a day for three days is the recommended dosage.

body as before. As each small area is commenced, a little baby powder can be sprinkled around the hair roots. As this is brushed and combed out, it will clean the fur, remove grease, and help to keep it tag free. Talcum powder can be used but it may cause irritation. Powdered chalk is another long-established alternative.

Finish by brushing with the lie of the coat; the hair should then be tag free. Now combing will be easier. A tip for show cat owners is that the use of powder in the coat is most advantageous in the lighter coat colours. Use powder sparingly in the darker ones. The chamois leather is better to polish the darker coat. It produces a better shine than if excess powder has been used.

COMBING

Combing should be done in the same manner as the brushing, except that the final comb need not be done with the lie in most varieties. Combing against the lie is a good opportunity to see if there are any parasites present. These often favour the tail base or the neck behind the ears. However, in the tabby it should be because this will best show off the pattern. If any mats should be found in the coat, these must be teased out using the index finger and thumb of both hands. Be very careful not to pull away from the skin while doing this. It will be painful and the cat will object. Never bath a cat that has even the smallest of mats in its fur. Once soaked these will shrink into a tight ball that will be much harder to tease apart.

BATHING

During the course of its life there will usually be a number of occasions when any cat will need a bath, this being more so for a longhaired breed. For the Persian show cat, this will normally be a necessity about seven days prior to a show.

Using the kitchen sink is preferable to a bath. This saves bending and allows for better control of the cat. To prevent the cat from sliding, use a rubber mat. A spray attachment is more efficient than a jug to wet and rinse the coat. The cat should have its own towels.

The choice of shampoo is important. It should ideally be formulated for cats—do not use

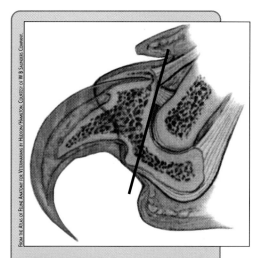

FROM THE ATLAS OF FELINE ANATOMY FOR VETERINARIANS BY HUDSON/HAMILTON, COURTESY OF W B SAUNDERS COMPANY

DECLAWING

Declawing is the surgical removal of all of the claw (or nail) and the first toe joint. This practice is heavily frowned upon and even illegal in some countries, such as the United Kingdom. Unfortunately, in some areas of the world this procedure is still performed. Some owners only have the claws from the front feet removed; others do all four feet. An alternative surgical procedure is removing the tendon that allows the cat to protract its claws. This procedure, referred to as a tendonectomy, as compared to an onychectomy (removal of the claws), is less traumatic for the cat. Claws still must be filed and trimmed after a tendonectomy.

Declawing is not always 100% successful. In two-thirds of the cases, the cats recovered in 72 hours. Only 4–5% of the cats hadn't recovered within a fortnight. About 3% of the cats had their claws grow back!

PRESS-ON NAILS!

A stylish and fairly successful inhibitor of scratching is to use a plastic covering on the nails. A plastic sheath is placed over each nail and glued on with a strong, permanent adhesive. Depending upon the cat's activity, these sheaths last from one to three months.

Start bathing your Persian before it is six months of age so it will become accustomed to the bathing process.

one for dogs. This could cause problems on a cat's coat. Baby shampoos are the best alternative. Dry shampoos in powder form are available from pet shops. Alternatives would be talcum powder, powdered chalk or heated bran flakes.

The kitten should be bathed by the time it is six months of age. This will familiarise it with the process before it matures and the process degenerates into a pitched battle. Cats have no love of bathing but can come to accept it if it does not become an unpleasant ordeal.

Grooming should always precede bathing, as this will remove any dead hairs. The key to

Dry your Persian with a quality towel to remove as much liquid as possible from the coat before using the dryer.

success lies in ensuring that no water or shampoo is allowed to enter and irritate the eyes or ears. You should be able to cope single-handedly with a kitten. However, it may be prudent to have someone else present just in case the kitty proves more of a super cat than a kitten!

The water temperature should be warm, never cold nor too hot.

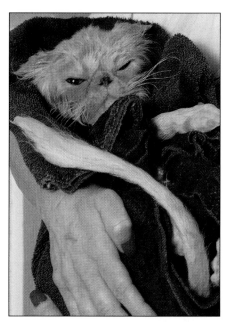

Prepare a shampoo and water solution before commencing. Have a large towel at hand. Commence by soaking the fur of the neck, then work along the back, sides, legs and tail. Pour shampoo onto the back and work this in all directions until the cat has been fully shampooed. Next,

Be careful of getting shampoo in the cat's eyes.

thoroughly rinse all the shampoo away. It is essential that none be left otherwise it may cause later irritation. The use of a hair conditioner is optional. Its main drawback is that it may make the coat too greasy within days of the bath. Gently but firmly squeeze all water from the coat. The face can be cleaned using a dampened flannel.

Give the cat a brisk rubbing to remove as much liquid as possible from the coat. Now the blaster can be used. Be very careful not to hold this too close to the fur otherwise it may burn the skin. Keep the nozzle on the move

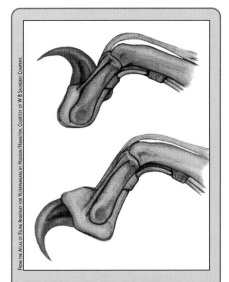

RETRACTABLE CLAWS

When at rest, a cat's claws are retracted. The muscles hold the claws in their sheaths. The claw is then extended if the cat wishes to attack prey, defend itself, grab an object or climb. That is why your cat's claws are not always visible. This is true for all species of felines except the cheetah, which is unable to retract its claws, except when it is very young.

CLEAN CATS

Cats are self groomers. They use their barbed tongue and front paws for grooming. Some cats never groom themselves, while others spend up to a third of their waking hours grooming themselves. Licking stimulates certain skin glands that make their coat waterproof.

continually. While drying, it is best to be grooming the coat at the same time. This will need the help of another family member to hold the cat while you dry and groom. If the drying process is done correctly, the cat will actually enjoy this part of its grooming once familiar with it.

When the cat is dry, it should be given a final good brushing,

Be extremely careful when cleaning around your Persian's eyes.

DRY SHAMPOO

A dry bath may be preferred to a wet one during very cold weather or when the cat is not well enough for a water bath. Sprinkle dry shampoo into the coat and give it a good brushing. This will remove excess grease and dirt without being as thorough as a wet bath. Be very sure all the powder is brushed from the fur to avoid potential irritation and consequential scratching.

of this with your thumb. The nail will appear from its sheath. If the nail needs trimming, use the appropriate trimmers.

It is vital you do not cut into, or even too close to, the quick, which is a blood vessel. This can be seen as a darker area of the nail

then kept indoors for a couple of hours to ensure it is thoroughly dry. Baby powder can be used before the final brushing. The Persian will now look and smell magnificent.

EARS, EYES AND NAILS

When inspecting the ears, look for any signs of dirt. This can be gently wiped away using a dampened cotton bud or one with just a little baby or vegetable oil on it. Never attempt to probe into the ear. If the ear is very waxed, this may indicate any of various health problems. A visit to the vet is recommended. The corner of the eyes can be gently wiped with damp cotton wool to remove any dust that occasionally accumulates.

Inspection of a cat's claws is achieved by firstly restraining it while on its back on your lap or held against your chest. Hold the paw and apply pressure to the top

CAT COATS

The long primary hairs of longhaired cats can be almost three times as long as those of a shorthaired cat. The genes for length of hair are independent of the genes for colour. The original colour of cats is the mackerel or tiger-striped pattern. This pattern was inherited from the ancestors of the housecat.

in pink-clawed cats. It is more difficult, or not possible, to see the quick in dark-coloured nails. In such instances trim less. You may need a helper to do the trimming or the holding. If in doubt, let your vet do this for you. If cats have ample access to scratching posts, they will only infrequently, if ever, require their nails to be trimmed.

GINGIVITIS (Plasmocytic-Lymphocytic Stomatitis)

There are many causes of this condition. But the end result is the same—bad breath, excessive plaque, tooth loss and almost certainly pain. The cat salivates excessively, starts to eat less, and consequently loses weight. On inspection, the gums are swollen, especially in the area of the premolar and molar teeth, and bleed easily. There are various treatments, such as antibiotics, immunostimulants and disinfectant mouth gel. However, these invariably prove short-term relief and merely delay the inevitable treatment of extraction.

Prevention avoids this painful condition. Regular tooth inspection and cleaning, plus provision of hard-food items, such as cat biscuits, achieve this to a large extent. There are also special cat chews made of dried fish that help clean the teeth. They also contain antibacterial enzymes that minimise or prevent secondary bacteria from accumulating. Ask for these at your pet shop or vet's surgery. Gingivitis may commence in kittens, so do not think it is something that only occurs in the older cat.

Never probe inside your cat's ear canal. Gently clean the ear with a dampened cotton bud.

TEETH

From its youngest days your kitten should become familiar with having its teeth cleaned. Many owners do not give these the attention they should. This has become progressively more important due to the soft diet regimens of modern cats. Initially, gently rub the kitten's teeth using a soft cloth on which toothpaste has been placed. This will accustom the kitten to having its teeth touched as well as to the taste of the tooth cleaner. When this is no problem for the kitten, you can progress to a soft toothbrush and ultimately one of medium hardness. Periodically let your vet check the cat's mouth.

Training and Behaviour of Your
PERSIAN CAT

SETTING THE GROUND RULES

From the outset you must determine the ground rules and stick to them. Always remember that your companion's patterns of behaviour begin to form from the moment it first arrives in your home. If the future adult is not to be given outdoor freedom, then do not let it outdoors as a kitten. If any rooms are to be out of bounds to the adult, then do not let the kitten into them. Stability is vital in a cat's life. When this is not so, the result will be stress and its related behavioural changes.

Ground rules of how to handle the kitten and to respect its privacy when sleeping should be instilled into all children. The cat's meals should be given at about the same time each day. This will have the secondary advantage that the pet's toilet habits will be more predictable.

One of the outstanding virtues of cats is that they are easy to live with. They are fastidious in their personal habits related to grooming and toilet routines and basically require very little of their owners. Nonetheless, behavioural problems in cats can occur, and an owner needs to understand all the possible causes and solutions. You may never encounter a single problem with your cat, but it pays to be prepared should your feline charge disrupt your domestic bliss.

THE BASIS OF TRAINING

The most effective means of training a cat is via reinforcement of success. A cat learning from lavish praise of doing what is required will want to repeat the action to gain more affection. There are no potential negative side effects. Conversely, when scolding or other methods of discipline are used, there is always the possibility the cat will not relate the punishment to what the owner had intended.

For example, you cannot discipline for something done in the past. The past is anything much longer than a few minutes ago. If you call the cat to you and punish it for something done hours earlier, it cannot relate to that action. It will relate the discipline to the act of going to you when called! This will create insecurity in the pet, increasing the risk that more problems will develop.

REMEDIAL METHODS

When faced with a problem, firstly try to pinpoint the likely cause(s). Next, consider the remedial options. Be sure these will not result in negative side effects linked to you. Always be the paragon of patience. Some problems may be extremely

CATS AND OTHER PETS

If you already have a pet cat or cats, or dogs, or almost any other animal that isn't small, creeping or crawling, your cat can usually be socialised so the other pet and the cat will tolerate each other. In many cases, cats and dogs become quite friendly and attached to each other, often making frequent physical contact, sleeping together or even sharing each other's food.

HAIR, HAIR EVERYWHERE

Cat's hairs grow denser on the abdomen than on the back. The hairs grow according to both light period-icity (daylight versus dark nights) and temperature. Outdoor cats living in colder climates cast their coats twice a year, in the spring and fall, while house cats do so all year long.

POSSIBLE CAUSES OF LITTERBOX PROBLEMS

1. The litter tray is dirty. Cats never like to use a previously fouled tray.
2. The litter has been changed to one of a different texture which the cat does not like. Generally the finer-grained litters are the most favoured.
3. A scented litter is being used to mask odours. The cat may not like the scent. Such litters should not be necessary if the tray is regularly cleaned.
4. The tray is regularly cleaned, but an ammonium or pine-based disinfectant is being used. This may aggravate the cat's sensitive nasal mucous membranes. Additionally, the phenols in pine are dangerous to cats.
5. The litter tray is located too close to the cat's food and water bowls. Cats do not like to eat near litter trays or to defecate/urinate close to their feeding area.
6. Another cat or free-roaming pet has been added to the household and is causing the cat to stress. In multi-cat households, two or more trays may be needed.
7. There is insufficient litter in the tray. There should be about 1 to 1.5 inches of litter depth.
8. The cat has developed a fear of using the tray due to an upsetting experience. For instance the owner may have caught the cat as it finished using the tray in order that it could be given a medicine. Children may be disturbing it while it is relieving itself.
9. The cat is ill (or elderly) and is unable to control its bowel movements. Veterinary attention is required.
10. The cat, because of one or more of the previous problems, has established other more favourable areas.

Litterbox training is essential for a housecat.

complex and deeply rooted within the cat's behaviour patterns. As such they are habits not easily changed, and often difficult to analyse. In discussing the following problems it is hoped you will understand the basic ways in which to correct other unwanted patterns of behaviour that might occur. But always remember it is far better to avoid a problem than correct it.

THE LITTER TRAY

A very common problem for some owners is that their cat starts to attend to its toiletry needs anywhere other than in its litter tray. The problem may become apparent from the time the kitten gets to its new home, or it may develop at any time during its life. So, let us start from the beginning and try to avoid the situation.

Until you are satisfied the

kitten is using its litter tray, do not give it access to carpeted rooms. The youngster should already have been litter trained well before you obtained it. You should obtain a litter tray similar to the one it is already familiar with. It is also important that the same brand of litter is used, at least initially. Place the tray in a quiet spot so the kitten has privacy when attending its needs.

A kitten will need to relieve itself shortly after it has eaten, exercised, or been sleeping. Watch it carefully at these times. If it stoops to attend to its needs other than in the litter tray, calmly lift it into its tray and scratch at the litter. Never shout or panic the kitty by making a sudden rush for it. If it does what is hoped, give it lots of

TIDY TOILETING

During the kitten's stay in the nest box, the mother will assist or even stimulate bowel and urine elimination, at least for the first month of the kitten's life. The mother also does the clean up work in the nest box. But once the kitten is older, it becomes capable of relieving itself out of the nest box. Usually the kitten likes sand, soft earth or something that seems absorbent and is easily moved with its paws. By the time the kitten is two months old, it should develop the discipline of covering its elimination. Not all kittens develop this discipline, though the use of an absorbent clay litter seems to be helpful in developing this discipline in young cats. Your local pet shop will have various cat litters to offer you.

Place your cat's litterbox in a private area with easy access for the cat.

praise. If it steps out of the tray, gently place it back in for a few seconds.

If nothing happens, be patient and wait, then repeat the process. If it fouls the kitchen floor when you are not watching, simply clean this up and wait for the next opportunity to transport the kitten to its tray. It rarely takes long for a kitten to consistently use this. Be very sure the tray is kept spotless. Cats have no more desire to use a fouled toilet than you do. Every few days give the cat tray a good wash using soapy water and always rinse it thoroughly. Allow it to dry then fill the tray with litter to depth of about 1–2 inches.

If your Persian stops using the litter tray, you must determine the reason why, such as the tray is dirty, the addition of another cat or even illness. By identifying the cause(s) of litter tray problems, the correction is often self-evident. However, once the cause has been addressed, this is only part of the solution. Next, the habit of fouling other places must be overcome. Where possible, do not let the cat enter rooms it has started to foul until the odour has had time to fully disperse. Wash the area of the fouling then treat carpets and soft

In multi-cat households, two or more litter trays are needed to prevent possible litterbox problems.

MAN MEETS CAT

Early man, perhaps 8000 years ago, started his symbiotic relationship with domestic cats, *Felis catus* or *Felis domesticus*. The cats killed and ate the rats and mice, and probably anything else which crawled and was small, which early man attracted and considered as pests. Early man reciprocated by allowing the cat to sleep in his cave, hut or tent. Cats, being essentially nocturnal, kept the small mammals (rats, mice, etc.) from disturbing the sleep of early man.

As early man evolved to modern man, the domestic cat came along as an aid to pest control. This was especially true of peoples who farmed, as farmers were plagued with rodents. Though most cats were not selectively bred for their predatory skills, it was obvious that those cats that were the best hunters were more successful in evolutionary terms than the cats that were more meek. Modern cats have changed very little from the cats from which they descended. There are still, today, cats that are very predatory, attacking small mammals and birds; there are also meek cats which, unless fed by their owners, would perish in a competitive cat society.

It has been shown repeatedly that if kittens are socialised in a proper manner, they will be peaceful pets. This includes lions and tigers. If the kittens are not socialised properly, they revert immediately to their aggressive predatory behaviours.

FERAL CATS

Free-roaming, near-wild cats are, as a general rule, undernourished. They spend most of their time searching for food. Consequently, those feral cats that have kittens spend less time with their kittens than well-nourished cats. It has been shown that kittens born to feral mothers are usually unsocial and show little affection for their mothers. Obviously, they would show a similar lack of affection for a human. That's one of the reasons that feral kittens make poor pets and should neither be adopted nor brought into your home. Kittens, which for any reason are separated from their mothers at the age of two weeks, develop an attitude of fear and wariness. They shun contact with other cats or humans, and can even be dangerous if they feel trapped.

furnishings with an odour neutraliser (not an air freshener) from your pet shop or vet.

If the cat cannot be prevented from entering certain rooms, then cover previously fouled areas with plastic sheeting or tinfoil. Also, place a litter tray in the fouled room while the retraining is underway. It may help if a different size, type or colour of tray is used.

POSSIBLE CAUSES OF SCENT MARKING

1. Another cat, or pet, has been introduced to the household. It may be bullying the resident cat. This problem may resolve itself when the two get to know each other. The more cats there are, the longer it may take for the situation to be resolved. Much will depend on the space within which the cats may roam and whether they are able to avoid those they dislike.
2. The birth of a new family member may annoy the cat for a while, especially if its owner suddenly gives it less attention.
3. A friend staying in the home for a few days may not like cats. If 'shooed' away a number of times, the cat may feel it should assert its position and mark it.
4. If the cat is given outdoor freedom, a bully may have moved into the territory. Having lost monopoly of its own garden, the pet may assert its territorial boundaries within its home. If a cat flap is used, another cat may be entering the home and this will trigger the resident to scent mark.

SCENT MARKING

Both sexes scent mark though males are more prolific. It is a means of advertising their presence in a territory, thus an integral part of their natural behaviour. Spraying is usually done against a vertical surface. It tells other males that the individual is residing in that territory and tells a female that a male lives close by. Likewise, a female's spraying will tell the male that a female is in the area. It is thus a very important part of a cat's social language.

Neutered cats have little need to mark their territory, or leave their 'calling' card to attract mates. They are far less likely to spray than those not altered. However, scent marking may commence when the cat is attempting to assert its position in the household.

To overcome the problem of scent marking, the first need is to try and identify if there is an obvious specific cause. In multi-cat households, it also requires positive identification of the sprayer(s) and the favoured spraying surface. Giving the cat more freedom may help, and its own sleeping place if it does not have one. Covering the sprayed surface with plastic sheeting, or a cloth impregnated with a scent the cat does not like (such as lemon, pepper or bleach) may be successful. Spraying the cat with a water pistol when catching it in the action is a common ploy. Veterinary treatment with the hormone progesterone may prove effective—discuss this with your vet.

SCRATCHING

Scratching is a normal feline characteristic. Unfortunately, house cats tend to destroy the furniture to satisfy their need to scratch. Feral or outdoor cats usually attack a tree because trees are readily accessible and the bark of the tree suits their needs perfectly. If the outdoor cat lives in a pride, it will scratch more than a solitary feral cat. The reasons for this are known. When cats scratch, they leave telltale marks. Parts of the nail's sheath, exudate from glands located between their claws, and the visual aspects are the marks which cats leave to impress or advertise their presence.

Cat owners whose cats scratch should not consider the scratching as an aggressive behavioural disorder. It is normal for cats to scratch. Keeping your cat's claws clipped or filed so they are as short as possible without causing bleeding may inhibit scratching. Your vet can teach you how to do this. Clipping and filing should be started when the kitten is very young. Starting this when the cat has matured is much more difficult and may even be dangerous.

There are ways to control annoying cat scratching. Certainly, the easiest way is to present your cat with an acceptable cat scratching post. These

MARKING TERRITORY

Cats are geographical by nature and they mark their territories in the usual way...by spraying their urine. The frequency of spraying is amazing! A non-breeding male cat that is not within its own turf will spray about 13 times an hour while travelling through the new territory. A breeding male will spray almost twice as much. One report states that free-ranging males spray 62.6 times an hour—that's more than once a minute!

Cat urine is recognisable for at least 24 hours and male cats spend a lot of time sniffing the area. Females spend less time but both sexes easily recognise the urine from male cats that are strange to the area.

CAT SCRATCH DISEASE

An objectionable habit of many poorly raised kittens is their exuberant jump to greet you. This flying jump must result in the kitten being attached to your body; otherwise it will fall to the floor and may injure itself. In the attachment process, your skin will usually be pierced and this is a health concern. All cat scratches and bites should be thoroughly cleaned with an antiseptic soap. If a sore appears at the site of the wound, you should visit your family doctor immediately.

Cat scratch disease is a well-known problem. It is caused by a bacterium *(Rochalimaea henselae)* that is usually easily treated with antibiotics. However, more and more cases show resistance to the usual antibiotics.

Untreated cat scratch fever may result in an enlargement of the lymph nodes, imitating a cancerous condition known as lymphoma. Interestingly enough, the lymph nodes, upon biopsy, may show large Reid-Sternberg cells, which are a characteristic of Hodgkins lymphoma. The bottom line is that cat scratches should be taken seriously.

are usually available at most local pet shops. The post should be covered with a material that is to your cat's liking. If your cat has already indicated what it likes to scratch, it usually is a good idea to cover the post with this same material. Veterinary surgeons often suggest that you use sandpaper, as this will reduce the cat's nails quickly and it will not have the urge to scratch. Certainly using hemp, carpeting, cotton towelling or bark is worth a try. Once the cat uses the post, it usually will have neither a desire nor a need to scratch any place else.

Besides the physical need to scratch, many cats have a psychological need to scratch. This is evidenced by where they scratch versus what they scratch. Often cats prefer semi-darkness. Some prefer flat surfaces and not vertical surfaces. Some prefer public areas in which their human friends are present instead of secretive areas. It may be stress related, as with scent marking, because scratching is another territorial marker behaviour. In any case the idea is to get your cat to scratch the post and not the carpets, furniture, drapes or the duvet on your bed.

Introduce your cat to the post by rubbing its paws on the post, hoping it will take the hint. Sometimes the cat voluntarily attacks the post. Unfortunately, usually it doesn't. If you catch your cat scratching in a forbidden area, startle it with a loud shout, banging a folded newspaper against your hand, or something which will take its attention away from scratching. Never hit the cat. This will only get a revengeful reaction that might be dangerous.

RUBBISH RUMMAGING

Cats are inquisitive and may decide to have a good look through any interesting rubbish bins that are exuding an enticing odour. Normally, the answer is to remove the bin. However, if the attraction always seems to be kitchen rubbish, there may be a nutritional problem. It may be searching for food because it is being underfed! It may alternatively be receiving an unbalanced diet and is trying to satisfy its inner need for a given missing ingredient.

Another possibility, and one which may be more appropriate to the indoors-only cat, is boredom or loneliness. These conditions can only be remedied by greater interaction between owner and cat and/or obtaining a companion feline.

Clearly the cause should be identified. The immediate solution is to place the rubbish in a cupboard or similar place that is out of the cat's reach. This type of solution is called removal of the re-enforcer. It is a common method of overcoming problems across a number of unwanted behaviours. However, it does not correct the underlying problem that must still be addressed.

The first-time cat owner should not think that the problems discussed would likely be encountered. They are only met when the cat's environment is lacking in some way. Always remember that the older cat may have problems with bowel control. An extra litter tray at another location in the home will usually remedy this situation. Finally, if a problem is found and you are not able to remedy it, do seek the advice of your vet or breeder.

SCRATCHING FURNITURE

All cats need to scratch in order to maintain their claws in good condition. For this reason, one or more scratching posts strategically placed in the cat's most used rooms will normally prevent the problem. Place the post in front of the scratched furniture. It can be moved steadily further away once the furniture is ignored. This is a problem that may become more manifest when cats are not allowed outdoors and have insufficient indoor opportunity to scratch.

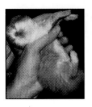

Breeding Your
PERSIAN CAT

TOO MANY CATS

There are already too many cats in the world. In too many countries, thousands of pathetic-looking felines can be seen wandering the streets in a badly emaciated state. They live tormented lives and have become a major social problem in many areas. There can be no excuse for these feral populations in developed Western nations. Quite frankly, some people who own cats, including some pedigree owners, lack a sense of responsibility.

Cats allowed to roam in a non-neutered state are by far the main reason for the overpopulation problem. Unless a cat is of show or breeding quality, there is not a single justification for it to be bred or to remain in a non-neutered state. If your Persian was purchased as a pet, you should help to resolve this global problem by having it neutered at the earliest possible date. This will make it a far healthier, better and less problematic pet.

While the idea of becoming a breeder may appeal to many owners, the reality is more difficult than is often appreciated. It requires dedication, considerable investment of time and money, and the ability to cope with many heart-wrenching decisions and failures.

It would be quite impossible to discuss the complexities of practical breeding in only one chapter, so we will consider the important requirements of being a breeder plus basic feline reproductive information. This will enable you to better determine if, indeed, this aspect of the hobby is for you.

BEING A BREEDER

Apart from great affection for the breed, a successful breeding programme requires quantifiable objectives. Foremost among these is the rearing of healthy kittens free from known diseases. Next is the desire to produce offspring that are as good as, indeed better than, their parents.

Such objectives ensure that a breeder will endeavour to maintain standards and reduce or remove from the cat population any instances of dangerous diseases and conditions. Only stock registered and tested free of

major diseases should ever be used. Adopting such a policy helps to counteract those who breed from inferior and often unhealthy cats.

To be a successful breeder you will need to become involved in the competition side of the hobby. Only via this route will you be able to determine if your programme is successful or not. Always remember that even the top winning breeders still produce quite a high percentage of kittens that will only be of pet quality. There will be many disappointments along the road to even modest success.

THE DISADVANTAGES OF BREEDING

There are many rewards to be gained from breeding but the disadvantages should also be carefully considered. Kittens are demanding, especially once they are over three weeks of age. Rearing, vaccination, registration and veterinary bills will be costly. Any thoughts of profit should be dispelled. Homes must be found for the kittens which will entail receiving many telephone calls–some at very inconvenient hours.

Many potential buyers will prove to be either unsuitable or 'time wasters' looking for the cheapest pedigreed cat obtainable. Kittens may die, while cats of any age could test positive for a major

TOM FOOLERY

A male cat kept as a single pet has little or no value for breeding purposes. It must be exhibited so it can gain some fame. The owner must have modern facilities to house both males and females. Females are always serviced at the home of the stud owner. This is extra responsibility and cost.

Such a male cannot be given any freedom to roam. If the tom is kept indoors, its scent marking odours will often become intolerable. Even kept outdoors in a suitable cat pen, it will spray regularly to attract the attention of any females in the area. Toms are more assertive and often more aggressive than neutered males.

If they are allowed any outdoor freedom, they will become involved in battles with the local toms. Consequently, they will soon lose their handsome looks! Most cat breeders do not even keep entire males because of the problems and costs they entail. These cats are best left in large catteries where the owners have the time, the funds, and everything else needed to justify their retention.

CAVEAT EMPTOR

When purchasing a kitten for breeding, make certain the seller knows what your intentions are. If a kitten is registered on the non-active register, this means it was not considered by its breeder to be good enough for breeding. Any kittens bred from such a cat cannot be registered. You should also check that the mother of the kitten/young adult you are interested in has tested negative for feline leukaemia and that all other vaccinations are current.

try to escape and mate with any local tom with a twinkle in his eye! Their scent and calls will attract roving Romeos who will gather near your home and involve themselves in a series of raucous battles. Holidays and matings will need to be planned around hoped-for litter dates. All in all, owning only one or two breeding females is a major commitment.

Before deciding whether breeding really is something you want to do, what would make good sense would be to neuter the pet and then become an exhibitor. When you have exhibited a number of times, your knowledge of cats will be greater, as will your contacts. You will be more aware of what quality is all about, and what it will cost for a well-bred female. It will be like an apprenticeship. Whether you then become a breeder, remain an exhibitor, or prefer life as a pet owner, you will be glad you heeded the words of advice given here.

disease. They may have to be put to sleep or given to a caring person who understands the problem.

Owning a number of cats will mean investing in cat pens. When females come into heat, they will

CAT CALLS

Females left in a non-spayed state are far more at risk from diseases and infections of the uterus. When in heat, the female becomes unusually affectionate and provocative. Her calls, a sound once heard never forgotten, can become extremely annoying if she is left unmated.

STOCK SELECTION

Stock selection revolves around health, quality, sex and age. Before these are discussed, it should be stated that many beginners unwisely rush this process. It is essential that ample time be devoted to researching from whom to purchase. This decision will influence a novice breeder's entire future endeavours.

HEALTH

Cats should only be obtained from a breeder whose stock has been tested negative for FeLV, FIP and FIV. The stock should be current on all vaccinations and worm treatments. Additionally, its blood type should be known so as to avoid incompatibility problems.

QUALITY

This must come in two forms. One is in the individual cat's appearance; the other is in its genetic ability to pass on the quality of its parents. The best way of obtaining these paired needs is to obtain initial stock from a breeder having a proven record of success in Persians, and with the colour you plan to start with. Being well acquainted with the breed's standard will be advantageous when seeking foundation stock. A female show cat attains her titles based on her appearance, but she may not pass on those looks to her offspring. Another cat that is very sound may pass on most of her

THE MALE STUD

The selection of a suitable stud should have been planned months before, as it can take some time to find the best male to use. It is preferred that the breeding lines of the stud are compatible with those of the female, meaning both pedigrees will carry a number of the same individuals in them. This is termed line-breeding. The ideal male will excel in those features that are considered weak in the female. You may read in other books that if a female is weak in a given feature, the

ideal stud will be the total opposite. However, this can be misleading.

If the female has an overly long tail, what you do not need is a stud with a short tail. Rather, his tail should be as near the ideal length as possible. Genetically, this will improve tail length in your line without introducing unwanted genetic variance in your stock. Compensatory matings, such as short tail to long tail, will create such variance. Once a male has been selected, ensure all his papers and vaccinations are in order. The female will be taken to the stud and left with him for a few days.

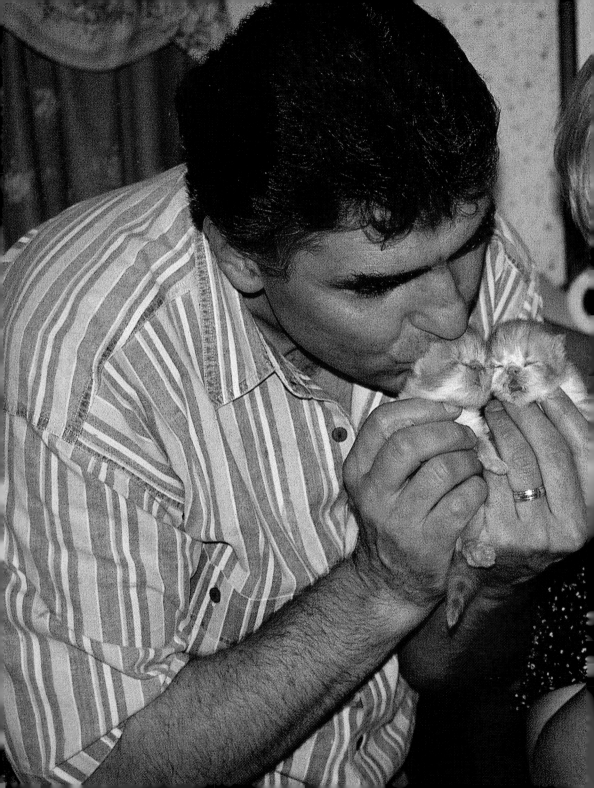

Start handling your kittens early on. This is the best kind of socialising. Socialising with humans is necessary for all housecats.

THE BREEDING QUEEN

A female used for breeding purposes is called a queen. The principal requirement of such a cat is that she is an excellent example of the breed. This does not mean she must be a show winner. Many a winning exhibition cat has proved to have little breeding value. This is because a show cat gains success purely on its appearance; however, it may not pass those looks to its offspring.

A good breeding female may lack that extra something needed to be a top winner. Yet, she may pass on most of her excellent features to her offspring. Much will depend on the breeding line from which she was produced. Therefore any potential breeder must research existing breeders to ascertain which have good track records of producing consistently high-quality Persian. In truth, and sadly, few newcomers in their haste to become breeders make this extra effort. This can result in becoming disillusioned if the female produces only average to inferior kittens.

good points and thus be more valuable for breeding. Of course, all litters will be influenced by the quality of the tom used. He will account for 50% of the offspring's genes. When viewing a litter of kittens, never forget that they are the result of the genes of two cats.

SEX

The beginner should only obtain females. The best advice is to commence with just one very sound female. By the time you have exhibited her and gained more knowledge about the finer points of the breed, you will be far better placed to judge what true quality is all about. By then you will also have made many contacts on the show circuit. Alternatively, you may decide breeding is not for you and will have invested the minimum of time and money. A male is not needed until a breeder has become established. Even then owning one is not essential to success. There is no shortage of quality studs. Males create many problems the novice can do without. Once experience is gained is the time to decide if owning a male would be of any particular benefit.

AGE

There is no specific age at which stock should be purchased but the following are suggested. 1. Most people purchase young kittens so they can enjoy them. However, with such youngsters their ultimate quality is harder to assess. 2. Chances are improved if a kitten has already won awards in shows. This will be when she is 14 weeks to 9 months of age, but she will be more costly. 3. A quality young female that has already produced offspring is a prudent choice but will be the most expensive option.

THE BREEDING PROCESS

Sexual maturity in cats may come as early as four months of age. Breeding should not be considered until the female is at least twelve months old, especially in the slow-maturing breeds such as those of Persian and European stock ancestry. A young cat barely out of her kitten stage may not have the required physical or psychological stability to produce and raise a vigorous litter. After her first heat, a female will normally come into heat again every two to three weeks and continue to do so until mated. The actual oestrus period lasts

ROAMING ROMEOS

Males cats, toms, have extended testicles, very early in life. Within about nine months the tom is capable of mating with a queen. Both queens and toms are polygamous and it is not uncommon for a queen to have a litter containing kittens fathered by different toms.

NEWBORN KITTENS

Most kittens are born with body hair. Their ears and eyes, however, remain closed for about two weeks, though some ears and eyes become functional after 72 hours. Kittens should be allowed to nurse for seven weeks, longer if they will not readily eat and drink from a plate. If allowed to nurse, most kittens will stay on their mother's milk for two months or more.

fourteen days. It is during this time that she is receptive to a male.

Once the mating has been successful, the time between fertil-isation and birth of the young, known as the gestation period, is in the range 59 to 66 days, 63 or 64 days being typical. The litter size will generally be two to five. Kittens are born blind and

THE HEAT IS ON

Most female cats reach sexual maturity by the time they are 28 weeks old. Females normally accept males from late winter to early fall, about a six-month period. They have a reproductive cycle of about two weeks and are in heat for about one of the two weeks. Intercourse causes the female to ovulate and pregnancy may last for about 66 days, perhaps longer in cold climates and shorter in the tropics.

helpless, but develop rapidly. Their eyes open about the seventh day. By 21 days they start exploring. At this time they will also be sampling solid foods. By eight weeks they can be vaccinated and neutered if required. Weaning normally commences by the age of six weeks and is completed within two to three weeks. Kittens can go

to a new home when 12 weeks old, though 14 to 16 is preferred. During this period you must decide if you wish to register the kittens or merely 'declare' them. This allows them to be registered at a later time. Obtain the necessary information and forms from your cat registration authority. You should also consider the benefits of registering your own breeder prefix. This, however, is only worthwhile if you intend to breed on a more than casual basis. If you have decided that certain kittens are unsuitable for showing/breeding, do consider early neutering.

WHAT'S A PEDIGREE WORTH?

When choosing breeding stock, never be dazzled by a pedigree. No matter how illustrious this is, it is only ever as good as the cat that bears it. If the cat is mediocre, then its prestigious pedigree is worthless from a breeding perspective. There are many other pitfalls for the novice when judging the value of a breeding line. These you must research in larger, more specialised books.

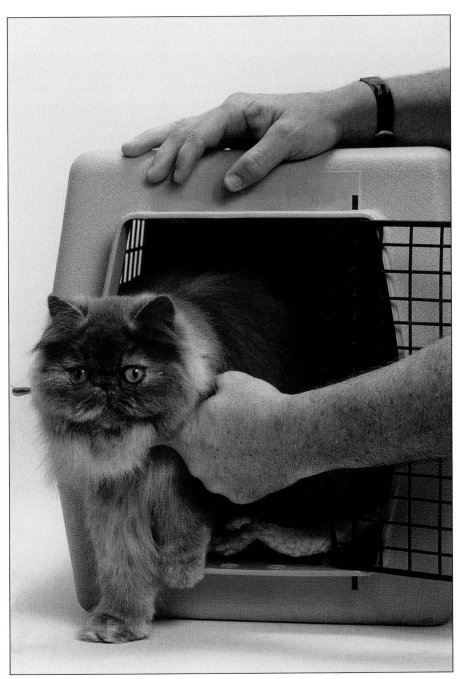

A crate or carrying box is a necessity if you intend to travel with your cat (even a trip to the vet is travelling). Train them early so they can feel comfortable when confined in the crate.

Kittens are born blind and deaf. It takes about a week for these two senses to function.

Exhibiting Your
PERSIAN CAT

CLASSES AT SHOWS

Open	Any cat of the specified breed.
Novice	Cats that have never won a first prize.
Limit	Cats that have not won more than first prizes.
Junior	Cats over nine months of age but less than two years on the day of the show.
Senior	Cats over two years old.
Visitors	Cats living a given distance away from the show venue.
Assessment	Experimenal breeds, but which have an approved standard.
Aristocrat	Cats with one or two Challenge Certificates (or premiers for neuters) so are not yet full champions/premiers.

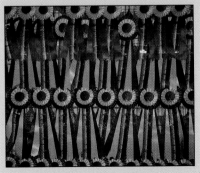

Without shows the cat fancy could not exist. There would be only a handful of breeds as compared with today's ever-growing list. There would be fewer colour patterns and far less cat awareness. Given the great importance of shows to the cat fancy, it is perhaps a little surprising, and disappointing, that the majority of cat owners have never visited a feline exhibition.

Shows such as the National and the Supreme of Britain, or their equivalents in other countries, are the shop windows of the world of domestic cats. They are a meeting place where breeders from all over the country compete to establish how well their breeding programmes are developing. A show is also a major social event on the cat calendar.

Whether a potential pet owner, or breeder of the future, you should visit one or two shows. It is a great day out for the whole family. Apart from the wonderful selection of breeds, there are also many trade stands. If a product is available, it will be seen at the large exhibitions.

Many of the national clubs

and magazines have stands. The two major shows mentioned are held in the winter months, usually November and December. However, there are hundreds of other shows staged during the year in various parts of the country. They range from small local club events to major championship breed shows and are usually advertised in the cat magazines. Your ruling cat association can also supply a list of shows.

SHOW ORGANISATION

So you will have some idea of how things are organised, the following information will be helpful. You will learn even more by purchasing the show catalogue. This contains the names and addresses of the exhibitors and details of their cats. It also lists the prizes, indicates the show regulations, and carries many interesting advertisements.

A major show revolves around three broad categories of cats:
1. Unaltered cats, meaning those that are capable of breeding.
2. Neuters.
3. Non-Pedigree cats.

There is thus the opportunity for every type of cat, from the best of Persians to the everyday 'moggie' pets, to take part. These three broad categories are divided into various sections. For example, the unaltered and neuters are divided into their

ON THE CONTINENT AND BEYOND...

In Britain the title of UK Grand Champion or Premier is won in competition with other Grand titleholders. In mainland Europe cats can become International Champions. More British cats are expected to become International Champions with the recent introduction of passports for cats, allowing cats to compete more freely on the Continent and beyond. In countries other than Britain, the way in which shows are organised and titles achieved do differ somewhat. However, they broadly follow the outline discussed here.

respective sections, such as Longhair, Semi-Longhair, British, Foreign, Siamese and so on.

There are many more classes other than those mentioned.

These include club classes and those for kittens and non-pedigree cats.

JUDGING

There are two ways cats can be judged. One is pen judging, the other is bench or ring judging. In Britain pen judging is the normal method, though bench judging is used for Best in Show. In pen judging the judge moves around the cat pens. The cat gaining the most points when compared to the standard wins. In bench judging, stewards take the cats to the judge.

If a cat wins its class, it then competes against other class winners. By this process of elimination, a cat may go on to win Best of Breed award. It then competes against other breed winners for the Best in Group award. The group winners compete for the Best in Show award.

A breeder can win a number of awards during the course of a show. Even those who do not own the very best cats can take pride in gaining second, third, fourth and recommended, especially if won at the larger shows. By progression the top cat at a show will win its class, its breed, its section, and ultimately become the Best in Show Exhibit. The titles a cat can win commence with that of Champion

Cats are judged in two ways: pen and bench. Usually pen judging is the method used, leaving bench judging for Best in Show.

In pen judging, the judge moves around the cat pens, which are often well decorated.

CATS SHOW STRESS

Stress reduces the effectiveness of the immune system. Seemingly innocuous conditions may develop into major problems or leave the cat more open to attack by disease. Stress is difficult to specifically identify, but its major causes are well known. These include incorrect diet, intrusion by another cat into its home or territory, excessive handling and petting, disturbed sleep, uncomfortable home temperatures, bullying by another cat or pet, parasitic infestation, boarding in a cattery, travel, moving home, boredom, limited accommodation space and, for some felines, being exhibited.

or Premier in the case of neuters. A Grand Champion is made after winning in competition with others of its same status. The same applies to a Grand Premier. The judging system may vary from one country to another but the basis remains as outlined.

THE SHOW CAT

When a cat is seen preening in its pen, the hard work that has gone into its preparation is rarely appreciated. Exhibits must be in peak condition and their coats in full bloom. The potential exhibit must be gradually trained to spend hours within its show pen. It must display no fear or aggression towards strangers, such as the stewards or the judges. These

Shows can last a long time, so make sure to bring toys to keep your cat entertained while waiting to be judged.

CLASSES FOR NON-PEDIGREE CATS

For non-pedigree cats there are many classes which include those for single colours, bicolours, tabbies, half pedigree, and so on. In this section are many delightful classes, such as those for cats owned by senior citizens, by young children (by age group), best original stray or rescued cat, best personality, most unusual looking, most photogenic, and best older cats. Within this cat section can be seen some truly gorgeous felines. There is no doubt that the pet classes have been the spring-board that has launched many a top breeder into the world of pedigree cats.

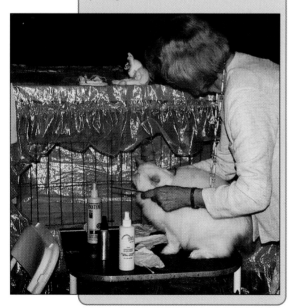

must be able to physically examine it, including its ears and teeth; it also involves being lifted into the air. If a cat scratches or bites a judge, or any other show official, it is automatically withdrawn from the show. A repeat of this in the future would result, in most instances, in the cat's show career being terminated by the ruling association.

Apart from being comfortable with people peering into its pen, the cat must be able to endure long journeys to the show venue. Unless trained, the cat may become a nervous, aggressive feline that will have a very short show career.

Obviously the cat must display quality. This means having none of the major faults that would prevent it from gaining a first prize. These are listed in the breed standard. The meaning of quality is very flexible. You do not need to own a potential champion to be a successful exhibitor. The cat must also be registered with the association under whose rules the show is being run. In Britain this will be the GCCF or The Cat Association of Britain.

As in anything competitive, exhibits can gain prizes at the lower levels of a hobby without having any realistic chance of awards in the major shows. Owning such exhibits is often part of a top breeder/exhibitor's portfolio from their early days in the hobby. Others may never move beyond the smaller shows but still gain reputations for owning sound stock. They thoroughly enjoy being involved at their given level.

If the idea of exhibiting appeals to you, the best way to make a start is to join a local club. There you not only will be advised on all procedures, but also will assuredly make many new friends. Exhibiting can be costly in cash and time, but you can focus on the more local shows while attending the larger ones as a visitor.

BECOMING AN EXHIBITOR

Before any hobbyist enters a show, he is advised to join a local cat club. Here, hobbyists will meet local breeders who will not only assess their cat for them, but also provide help on many other topics. The novice exhibitor could attend one or two shows with an exhibitor in order to learn the ropes. During this period, he can become familiar with the show rules and regulations. These are quite extensive, intended to safeguard the best interests of the hobby, the exhibitors and, most important, the cats.

It is of interest to note that some breeders own cats in partnership with other fanciers. This is useful when one person enjoys the breeding and the other the exhibition side. It enables both to really be involved in the hobby to a level that might not have been possible for either on his own. So, whether you fancy being an exhibitor or just love cats, do make a point of visiting the next major show in your area. You may just find the experience addictive!

Cats shows are colourful, enjoyable and educational affairs.

Health Care of Your
PERSIAN CAT

Maintaining a cat in the peak of good health revolves around the implementation of a sound husbandry strategy. At the basic level, this means being responsible about feeding, cleanliness and grooming. However, in spite of an owner's best efforts in these matters, cats may still become ill due to other causes. Although owners can attempt to prevent, identify and react to problems, only a vet is qualified to diagnose and suggest and/or effect remedies. Attempts by owners or 'informed' friends to diagnose and treat for specific diseases are dangerous and potentially life-threatening to the cat.

A LONG, HEALTHY LIFE

As veterinary surgeons make medical advances in the health care of cats, the longevity of the typical house cat is improving. Certainly ages between 15 and 18 years are not uncommon, and reports of cats living more than 20 years are forthcoming.

SELECTING A VETERINARY SURGEON

Your selection of a veterinary surgeon should not be based upon personality (as most are) but upon convenience to your home. You want a vet who is close because you might have emergencies or need to make multiple visits for treatments. You want a vet who has services that you might require such as nail clipping and bathing, as well as sophisticated pet supplies and a good reputation for ability and responsiveness. There is nothing more frustrating than having to wait a day or more to get a response from your veterinary surgeon.

All veterinary surgeons are licensed and their diplomas and/or certificates should be displayed in their waiting rooms. There are, however, many veterinary specialities that usually require further studies and internships. There are specialists in heart problems (veterinary cardiologists), skin problems (veterinary dermatologists), teeth and gum problems (veterinary dentists), eye problems (veterinary ophthalmologists) and x-rays (veterinary radiologists), as well as vets who have specialities in reproduction, nutrition and behaviour. Most veterinary surgeons do routine surgery, such as neutering and stitching up wounds. When the problem affecting your cat is serious, it is not unusual or impudent to get another medical opinion, although in Britain you are obliged to advise the vets concerned about this. You might also want to compare costs among several veterinary surgeons. Sophisticated health care and veterinary services can be very costly. Important decisions are sometimes necessarily based upon financial considerations.

PREVENTATIVE MEDICINE

It is much easier, less costly and more effective to practise preventative medicine than to fight bouts of illness and disease. Properly bred kittens come from

---

KEEPING YOUR CAT HEALTHY

Although there are a multitude of ailments, diseases and accidents that could befall a cat, all but the most minor of problems can be avoided with good management. The following tips are a recipe for keeping your cat in the best of health.

• Make sure it is vaccinated and in other ways protected from each of the major diseases. It must also receive annual boosters to maintain immunity.

• Have periodic checks made by your vet to see if your cat has worms.

• Ensure the cat receives an adequate diet that is both appealing and balanced.

• Have the kitten neutered if it is not to be used for breeding.

• Ensure the cat's litter tray, food/water vessels and grooming tools are always maintained in spotless condition.

• Do not let your cat out overnight or when you are away working or shopping.

• Always wash your hands after gardening or petting other people's pets.

• Groom your cat daily. If this is done, you will more readily notice fleas or other problems than if grooming was done less frequently.

• Never try to diagnose and treat problems that are clearly of an internal type. Remember, even the most informed of breeders is not a vet and unable to reliably diagnose problems for you or suggest treatments. Contact your vet.

• If you are ever in doubt about the health of your cat, do not delay in discussing your concerns with your vet. Delays merely allow problems to become more established.

A DELICATE HEART

A cat's heart is as delicate as a human's heart, but it is much smaller. At full maturity, queens' hearts weigh between 9-12 grammes. Toms' hearts are heavier, weighing 11-18 grammes. The blood that circulates through the heart chambers does not supply the heart muscle which requires a separate circulatory system.

parents who were selected based upon their genetic disease profile. Their mothers should have been vaccinated, free of all internal and external parasites and properly nourished. For these reasons, a visit to the veterinary surgeon who cared for the queen is recommended. The queen can pass on disease resistance to her kittens, which can last for eight to ten weeks. She can also pass on parasites and many infections. That's why you should visit the veterinary surgeon who cared for the queen.

VACCINATIONS

Most vaccinations are given by injection and should only be done by a veterinary surgeon. Both he and you should keep a record of the date of the injection, the identification of the vaccine and the amount given. The first vaccination is normally given when the kitten is about 8–9 weeks old. About 30 days later a booster is given. Although there are many diseases a cat may fall victim to, the most dangerous three—FIE, FVR and FeLV—can be safeguarded against with a single (three in one) injection. Thereafter an annual booster is all that is required.

MAJOR DISEASES

There are a number of diseases for which there is either no cure or little chance of recovery. However,

THE RIB CAGE

Cats usually have 13 pairs of ribs. The ribs in the middle are longer than the ribs on either end (or beginning) of the rib cage. The first nine ribs are joined to the chest bone (sternum) with costal cartilages. Ribs 10, 11 and 12 are also associated with cartilage, which contributes to the costal arch. The thirteenth rib is called the floating rib and its cartilage is separate from the other ribs.

BLOOD GROUP INCOMPATIBILITY (BGI)

In recent years blood group incompatibility has become the focus of scientists, vets and breeders. Its importance to pet owners is when transfusions are needed. For breeders it probably accounts for a large percentage of kittens that die from fading kitten syndrome. Scientifically the problem is called neonatal erythrolysis, meaning the destruction of red blood cells in newly born offspring.

Cats have two blood groups, A & B. Group A is dominant to B (which is genetically called recessive). When the antibodies of B group mothers are passed to A group kittens, via her colostrum milk, they destroy red blood cells. Death normally follows within a few days.

Most domestic cats tested are group A. However, national and regional differences display a variation in which 1-6% may be of type B. In pedigree breeds it has been found that the number of group B cats varies significantly. The following breeds, based on present available data, have the indicated percentage incidence of group B blood type.

0%	Siamese, Burmese and Oriental Shorthair
1-5%	Maine Coon, Manx and Norwegian Forest
10-20%	Abyssinian, Birman, Japanese Bobtail, Persian, Scottish Fold and Somali
25-50%	British Shorthair, Devon and Cornish Rex and Exotic Shorthair

The clear implication to breeders is to establish their cats' blood group, via testing, and conduct appropriate matings. These should not result in B group mothers nursing A group kittens. The safe matings are:

1. Group A males   x   A females
2. Group B males   x   A or B females
3. Group A females   x   A or B males
4. Group B females   x   B males

Breeders are advised to seek further information before embarking on stock purchase and breeding programmes.

some can be prevented by vaccination. All breeders and owners should ensure kittens are so protected.

FELINE INFECTIOUS ENTERITIS (FIE)
This is also known as feline panleukopenia and feline distemper. The virus attacks the intestinal system. It is spread via the faeces and urine. The virus may survive for many years in some environments. The use of household bleach (sodium hypochlorite) for cleaning helps to prevent colonisation. Signs, among others, are diarrhoea, vomiting, depression, anorexia and dehydration. Death may occur within days. A vaccine is available.

TAKE CARE OF THOSE KIDNEYS
The kidney of the cat is larger than that of the dog, but it has the typical bean shape. It receives 25% of the blood output of the heart! For this reason it has rather significant veins to accommodate this large supply of blood, and injuries suffered by the kidneys are usually serious and may be frequent.

FELINE VIRAL RHINOTRACHEITIS (FVR) & CALICIVIRUS (FCV)
Also known as cat flu this is a complex of upper respiratory diseases. Signs are excessive hard sneezing, runny nose and mouth ulcers. Cats vaccinated after having contracted flu may recover

HEALTH AND VACCINATION SCHEDULE

AGE	6 WKS	8 WKS	10 WKS	12 WKS	16 WKS	6 MOS	1 Y
Worm Control	✔	✔	✔		✔		
Neutering						✔	
Rhinotracheitis	✔	✔		✔	✔		✔
Panleukopenia	✔	✔		✔			✔
Calicivirus		✔			✔		✔
Feline Leukaemia				✔			✔
Feline Infectious Peritonitis				✔	✔		✔
Faecal Evaluation						✔	
Feline Immunodeficiency testing							✔
Feline Leukaemia testing				✔			✔
Dental Evaluation		✔				✔	
Rabies				✔	✔		✔

Vaccinations are not instantly effective. It takes about two weeks for the cat's immune system to develop antibodies. Most vaccinations require annual booster shots. Your veterinary surgeon should guide you in this regard.

DISEASE REFERENCE CHART

	What is it?	Cause	Symptoms
Feline Leukaemia Virus (FeLV)	Infectious disease; kills more cats each year than any other feline infectious disease.	A virus spread through saliva, tears, urine and faeces of infected cats; bite wounds.	Early on no symptoms may occur, but eventually infected cats experience signs from depression and weight loss to respiratory distress. FeLV also suppresses immune system making a cat susceptible to almost any severe chronic illness.
Rabies	Potentially deadly virus that infects warm-blooded mammals. Not seen in the United Kingdom.	A bacterium, which is often carried by rodents, that enters through mucous membranes and spreads quickly throughout the body.	Aggressiveness, a blank or vacant look in the eyes, increased vocalization and/or weak or wobbly gait.
Panleukopenia aka Kitty Distemper or Feline Parvovirus	Highly contagious virus, potentially deadly.	Ingestion of the virus, which is usually spread through the faeces of infected cats.	Most common: severe diarrhoea. Also vomiting, fatigue, lack of appetite, severe inflammation of intestines.
Feline Viral Rhinotracheitis (FVR)	Viral disease that affects eyes and upper respiratory tracts.	A virus that can affect any cat, especially those in multiple-cat settings.	Sneezing attacks, coughing, drooling thick saliva, fever, watery eyes, ulcers of mouth, nose and eyes.
Feline Immuno-deficiency Virus (FIV)	Virus that reduces white blood cells.	An infection spread commonly through cat fight wounds.	Signs may be dormant for years or innocuous, such as diarrhoea or anemia.
Feline Infectious Peritonitis (FIP)	A fatal viral disease, may be linked to FeLV and FIV.	Bacteria in dirty litter boxes; stress may increase susceptibility in kittens.	Extremely variable; range from abdominal swelling to chest problems, eye ailments and body lesions.
Feline Urological Syndrome (FUS)	A disease that affects the urinary tract of cats.	Inflammation of bladder and urethra.	Constipation, constant licking of penis or vulva, blood in urine (males), swollen abdomen, crying when lifted.

CLEANLINESS IS THE KEY

Crucial to the prevention and spread of disease is the need to maintain meticulous cleanliness, especially relating to the litter tray. Many diseases and problems are transferred via faecal matter. Once a problem is suspected, the advice of a vet should be sought. Blood tests, faecal microscopy and other testing methods are now available. They can make the difference between life and death for a cherished pet.

but may suffer recurrent bouts, especially if they become stressed.

FELINE LEUKAEMIA VIRUS (FELV)
This is a highly infectious viral disease. It is spread via direct contact—mutual grooming, saliva, feeding bowls, faeces, urine and biting. It can be passed prenatally from a female to her offspring. It creates tumours, anaemia, immune system depression, pyrexia (high temperatures), lethargy, respiratory disease,

NEUTERING

Neutering is a major means of avoiding ill health. It dramatically reduces the risk of males becoming involved in territorial battles with the dangers of physical injury and disease transference. It makes the male more placid and less likely to scent mark its home. It also reduces the incidence of prostate problems and there is no risk of testicular cancer. The female avoids potentially lethal illnesses related to her being allowed to remain in an unmated condition, such as breast cancer.

Neutering is usually performed between six and four months of age but it can be done as early as eight weeks of age. Data available on the age at which a kitten is neutered indicates that early neutering has more advantages than drawbacks. Breeders should have this performed on all cats sold as pets.

Male cats are neutered. The operation removes the testicles and requires that the cat be anaesthetised. Females are spayed. This is major surgery during which the ovaries and uterus are removed. Both males and females should be kept quiet at home for about seven to ten days following the procedure, at which time the vet will remove the sutures.

intestinal disease and many other potentially fatal problems. It is most prevalent in high-density cat populations. Not all cats will be affected, but they may become carriers.

Kittens less than six months old are especially vulnerable. Infected cats usually die by the time they are three to four years old. Cats can be screened or tested for this disease. Vaccination is not 100% effective but is recommended in kittens being sold into multi-cat environments.

FELINE IMMUNODEFICIENCY VIRUS (FIV)

This causes the white blood cells to be significantly reduced, thus greatly suppressing the efficiency of the immune system. It is not transferable to humans. Infection is normally gained from cat fight wounds; thus, outdoor males are at the most risk. A cat diagnosed via blood tests as FIV positive may live a normal life for months or years if retained indoors and given careful attention. Signs may be innocuous in the early stages, such as anaemia or diarrhoea. No vaccine is available.

FELINE INFECTIOUS PERITONITIS (FIP)

This viral disease is invariably fatal once contracted in its more potent forms. However, the virulence of the virus is variable and may by destroyed by the immune system. Stress may increase susceptibility in kittens. It may be linked to FeLV and FIV. Signs are extremely variable and range from abdominal swelling to chest problems, eye ailments to body lesions. There are various tests available but none is as yet 100% conclusive. Strict cleanliness is essential, especially of litter trays. No vaccine is available.

FELINE UROLOGICAL SYNDROME (FUS)

This is a very distressing condition caused by an inflammation of the bladder and urethra. Signs are constipation-like squatting and attempts to urinate, regular licking of the penis or vulva, blood in urine (males), swollen abdomen, crying when lifted and urinating in unusual places (often only small amounts).

The numerous causes include infection, dirty litter tray of the indoor cat, alkaline urine (in cats it should be acidic), diet too dry, lack of water intake (even though this may be available) and being hit by a vehicle (damaged nerves). Veterinary treatment is essential or the condition could be fatal due to bladder bursting or presence of dangerous bacteria.

RABIES

Britain and most European Community countries are free of this terrible disease. The stringent

THE PICA SYNDROME
The term pica is a veterinary term that refers to a morbid desire to ingest things that are abnormal to the cat's diet. Cats are usually addicted to soft materials like wool, silk, cotton or a mixture of these and synthetic cloths. Hard plastics, wood and even metals have been involved in this pica syndrome. If you observe your cat chewing these fabrics or materials, speak to your vet. Most veterinary surgeons who observe the pica syndrome think it is a nervous problem that can successfully be treated with drugs normally used for depression. In any case, the genetic makeup of your cat should be investigated and if pica occurs with any of the parents or previous offspring, do not breed your cat.

quarantine laws of Britain are such that vaccination is not necessary. However, the introduction of passports for dogs and cats means that resident British cats must be vaccinated if they are to travel abroad and return to the UK without being

HEALTHY CAT

In the United States, there are more cats than dogs. This has stimulated the veterinary medical community to learn more about cats and to prescribe more modern medicines to keep felines healthier.

placed into quarantine. The vaccination is given when the kitten is three or more months old. The pet passport process takes at least six months to complete, so plan well ahead.

COMMON HEALTH PROBLEMS

DERMATITIS (ECZEMA)

Dry lifeless coat, loss of coat, tiny scabs over the head and body, loose flakes (dandruff) and excessive scratching are all commonly called eczema. The cause covers a range of possibilities including diet,

parasitic mites such as *Cheyletiella spp*, fungus or an allergy to flea or other bites. Sometimes reasons are unknown. Veterinary diagnosis and treatment are required.

RINGWORM (DERMATOPHYTOSIS)

This problem is fungal, not that of a worm. The most common form is *Microsporum canis*, which accounts for over 90% of

POSSIBLE SOURCES OF EAR PROBLEMS

- Fight scratches
- Excess secretion of wax
- Swellings and blood blisters (haematoma) resulting from intrusion by foreign bodies (grass, etc.)
- Sunburn
- Whitish-coloured ear mites (*Otodectes cynotis*)
- Orange-coloured harvest mites (*Trombicula autumnalis*)
- Fleas
- Bacterial infection of either the outer or middle/inner ear

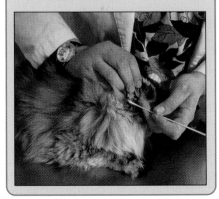

When cleaning your cat's ears, check carefully for mites or other signs that something could be wrong.

cases. Cats less than one year old are at the highest risk, while longhaired breeds are more prone to the problem than shorthaired cats. The fungi feed on the keratin layers of the skin, nails and hair. Direct contact and spores that remain in the environment are the main means of transmission.

Typical signs are circular-type bold areas of skin, which may be flaked and reddish. The coat generally may become dry and lifeless, giving the appearance of numerous other skin and hair problems. Veterinary diagnosis and treatment, either topical or via drugs, is essential as the condition is zoonotic. This means it can be transferred to humans.

EAR PROBLEMS

Most of the common ear problems affect the outer ear. Recognition is by the cat's constant scratching of

Dry skin can be a symptom of a serious problem.

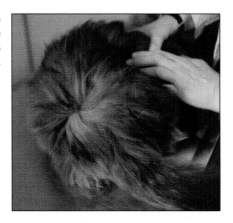

the ears and/or its holding the ear to one side. Greasy hairs around the ear, dark brown wax (cerumen) in the ears, scaly flakes in or around the ear or minute white or orange pinhead-like bodies (mites) in the ear are common signs. Canker is a term used for ear infections, but it has no specific meaning.

Over-the-counter remedies for ear problems are ineffective unless correct diagnosis has been made. It is therefore better to let the vet diagnose and treat the cat. Some problems may require anaesthesia and minor surgery.

DIARRHOEA
This is a general term used to indicate a semi to liquid state of faecal matter. Mild to acute cases may be due to a change of home, dietary change, eating an 'off' item, gorging on a favoured food, stress or a minor chill. These often rectify themselves within

days. Chronic and persistent diarrhoea may be the result of specific diseases. Any indication of blood in the faecal matter must be considered dangerous.

In minor cases, withholding food for 12–24 hours, or feeding a simple diet, may arrest the condition. If not, wisdom suggests contacting your vet. Faecal analysis and blood testing may be required. By answering numerous questions related to the cat's diet, general health, level of activity, loss of appetite, etc., the vet will determine whether tests are required or if immediate treatment seems more appropriate. Do not give cats human or canine intestinal remedies; these could prove dangerous.

CONSTIPATION
When a cat strains but is unable to pass motions, this is indicative of many causes. It may have hairballs, may have eaten a bird or rodent and has a bone lodged in its intestinal tract, may be suffering from a urological problem rather than constipation, or may have been hit by a car and has damaged the nerves that control bowel movements. As constipation is potentially serious, veterinary advice should be sought. Laxatives and faecal softener tablets may be given; the faecal matter can be surgically removed or other treatment carried out.

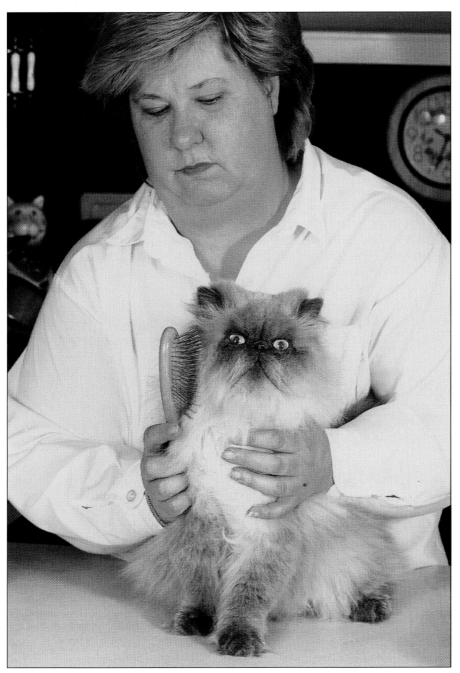

Regular grooming of your Persian will alert you to any possible health problems.

EXTERNAL PARASITES

Of all the problems to which cats are prone, none is more well known and frustrating than fleas. Indeed, flea-related problems are the principal cause of visits to veterinary surgeons. Flea infestation is relatively simple to cure but difficult to prevent. Periodic flea checks for your cat, conducted with annual health check-ups, are highly recommended. Consistent dosing with anthelinintic preparations is also advised. Parasites that are harboured inside the body are a bit more difficult to eradicate but they are easier to control.

FLEAS

To control a flea infestation you have to understand the flea's life cycle. Fleas are often thought of as a summertime problem but centrally heated homes have changed the patterns and fleas can be found at any time of the year. Fleas thrive in hot and humid environments; they soon die if the temperature drops below 2°C (35°F). The most effective method of flea control is a two-stage approach: one stage to kill the adult fleas, and the other to control the development of pre-adult fleas. Unfortunately, no single active ingredient is

A scanning electron micrograph (S. E. M.) of a flea.

S. E. M. BY DR DENNIS KUNKEL, UNIVERSITY OF HAWAII

Magnified head of a flea.

S. E. M. BY DR DENNIS KUNKEL, UNIVERSITY OF HAWAII

A Look at Fleas

Fleas have been around for millions of years and have adapted to changing host animals.

They are able to go through a complete life cycle in less than one month or they can extend their lives to almost two years by remaining as pupae or cocoons. They must have a blood meal every 10-14 days and egg production begins within two days of their first meal. The female cat flea is very prolific and can lay 2000 eggs in her lifetime!

They have been measured as being able to jump 300,000 times and can jump 150 times their length in any direction including straight up. Those are just a few of the reasons why they are so successful in infesting a cat!

PHOTO BY JEAN CLAUDE REVY/PHOTOTAKE

effective against all stages of the life cycle.

LIFE CYCLE STAGES
During its life, a flea will pass through four life stages: egg, larva, pupa and adult. The adult stage is the most visible and irritating stage of the flea life cycle and this is why the majority of flea-control products concentrate on this stage. The fact is that adult fleas account for only 1% of the total flea population, and the other 99% exist in pre-adult stages, i.e. eggs, larvae and pupae. The pre-adult stages are barely visible to the naked eye.

THE LIFE CYCLE OF THE FLEA
Eggs are laid on the cat, usually in quantities of about 20 or 30, several times a day. The female adult flea must have a blood meal before each egg-laying session. When first laid, the eggs will not cling to the cat's fur, as the eggs are not sticky. They will immediately fall to the floor or ground, especially if the cat moves around or scratches.

Once the eggs fall from the cat onto the carpet or furniture, they will hatch into yellow larvae, approximately 2 mms long. This takes from 5 to 11 days. Larvae are not particularly mobile, and

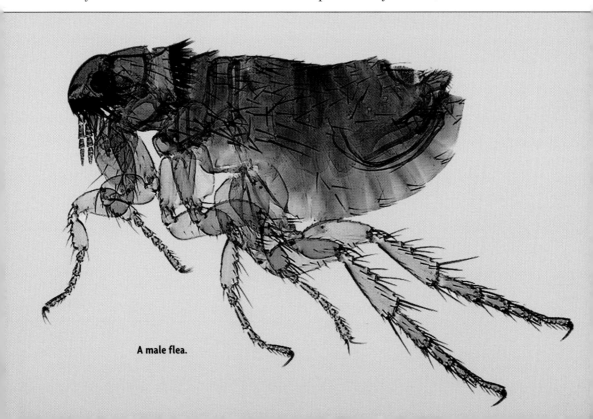

A male flea.

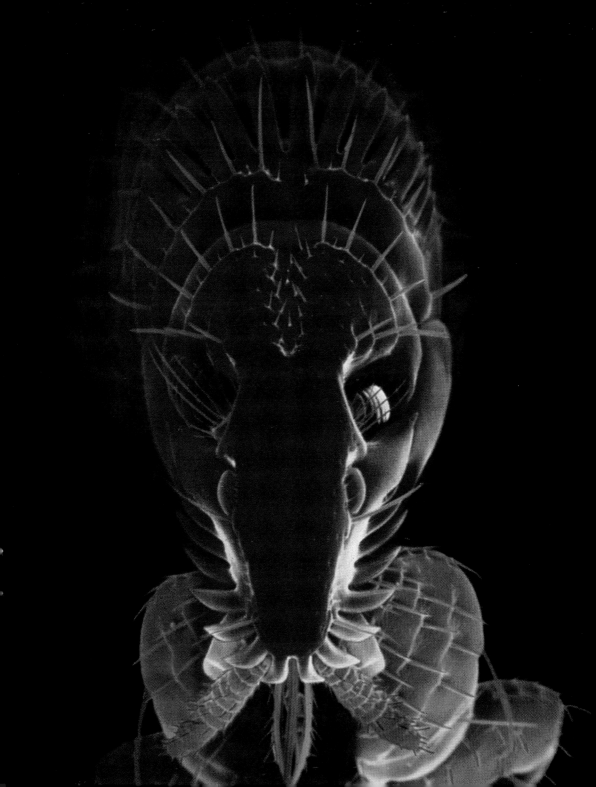

will usually travel only a few inches from where they hatch. However, they do have a tendency to move away from light and heavy traffic—under furniture, in the carpet and behind doors are common places to find high quantities of flea larvae.

The flea larvae feed on dead organic matter, including adult flea faeces, until they are ready to change into adult fleas. Fleas will usually remain as larvae for around seven days becoming darker in colour. After this period, the larvae will pupate a protective cocoon. While inside the pupae, the larvae will undergo metamorphosis and change into adult fleas. This can happen within a week, but the adult fleas can remain inside the pupae waiting to hatch for up to 6 months. The pupae are signalled to hatch by certain stimuli, such as physical pressure—the pupae's being stepped on, heat from an animal lying on the pupae or increased carbon dioxide levels and vibrations—indicating that a suitable host is available.

DID YOU KNOW?
Never mix flea control products without first consulting your veterinary surgeon. Some products can become toxic when combined with others and can cause serious or fatal consequences.

DID YOU KNOW?
Flea-killers are poisonous. You should not spray these toxic chemicals on areas of a cat's body that he licks, on his genitals or on his face. Flea killers taken internally are a better answer, but check with your vet in case internal therapy is not advised for your cat.

Once hatched, the adult flea must feed within a few days. Once the adult flea finds a host, it will not leave voluntarily. It only becomes dislodged by grooming or the host animal's scratching. The adult flea will remain on the host for the duration of its life unless forcibly removed.

TREATING THE ENVIRONMENT AND THE CAT

Treating fleas should be a two-pronged attack. First, the environment needs to be treated; this includes carpets and furniture, especially the cat's bedding and areas underneath furniture. The environment should be treated with a household spray containing an Insect Growth Regulator (IGR) and an insecticide to kill the adult fleas. There are also liquids, given orally, that contain chitin inhibitors. These render flea eggs incapable of development. There are both foam and liquid wipe-on treatments. Additionally, cats can

Opposite page: A scanning electron micrograph of a flea magnified more than 100x. This image has been colorized for effect.

S. E. M. BY DR DENNIS KUNEL, UNIVERSITY OF HAWAII

The Life Cycle of the Flea

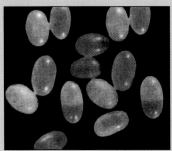

Eggs

Larva

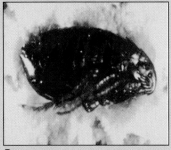

Pupa

Adult

Photos courtesy of Fleabusters® Rx for Fleas.

Flea Control

IGR (INSECT GROWTH REGULATOR)

Two types of products should be used when treating fleas—a product to treat the pet and a product to treat the home. Adult fleas represent less than 1% of the flea population. The pre-adult fleas (eggs, larvae and pupae) represent more than 99% of the flea population and are found in the environment; it is in the case of pre-adult fleas that products containing an Insect Growth Regulator (IGR) should be used in the home.

IGRs are a new class of compounds used to prevent the development of insects. They do not kill the insect outright, but instead use the insect's biology against it to stop it from completing its growth. Products that contain methoprene are the world's first and leading IGRs. Used to control fleas and other insects, this type of IGR will stop flea larvae from developing and protect the house for up to seven months.

EN GARDE:
CATCHING FLEAS OFF GUARD!

Consider the following ways to arm yourself against fleas:
• Add a small amount of pennyroyal or eucalyptus oil to your cat's bath. These natural remedies repel fleas.
• Supplement your cat's food with fresh garlic (minced or grated) and a hearty amount of brewer's yeast, both of which ward off fleas.
• Use a flea comb on your cat daily. Submerge fleas in a cup of bleach to kill them quickly.
• Confine the cat to only a few rooms to limit the spread of fleas in the home.
• Vacuum daily...and get all of the crevices! Dispose of the bag every few days until the problem is under control.
• Wash your cat's bedding daily. Cover cushions where your cat sleeps with towels, and wash the towels often.

be injected with treatments that can last up to six months. Emulsions that have the same effect can also be added to food. The advanced treatments are only available from veterinary surgeons. The IGRs actually mimic the fleas' own hormones and stop the eggs and larvae from developing into adult fleas. There are currently no treatments available to attack the pupa stage of the life cycle, so the adult insecticide is used to kill the newly hatched adult fleas before they find a host. Most IGRs are active for many months, while adult insecticides are only active for a few days.

PHOTO BY DWIGHT R KUHN

Dwight R Kuhn's magnificent action photo showing a flea jumping.

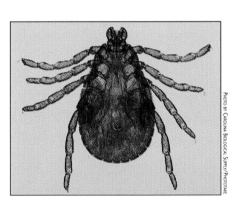

PHOTO BY CAROLINA BIOLOGICAL SUPPLY/PHOTOTAKE

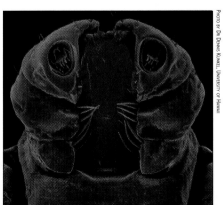

PHOTO BY DR DENNIS KUNKEL, UNIVERSITY OF HAWAII

When treating with a household spray, it is a good idea to vacuum before applying the product. This stimulates as many pupae as possible to hatch into adult fleas. The vacuum cleaner should also be treated with a flea treatment to prevent the eggs and larvae that have been hoovered into the vacuum bag from hatching.

The second stage of treatment is to apply an adult insecticide to the cat usually in the form of a collar or a spray. Alternatively, there are drops that, when placed on the back of the animal's neck, spread throughout the fur and skin to kill adult fleas. A word of warning: Never use products sold for dogs on your cat; the result could be fatal.

A brown cat tick, *Rhipicephalus sanguineus*, is an uncommon but annoying tick found on cats.

The head of a tick, *Dermacentor variabilis*, enlarged and coloured for effect.

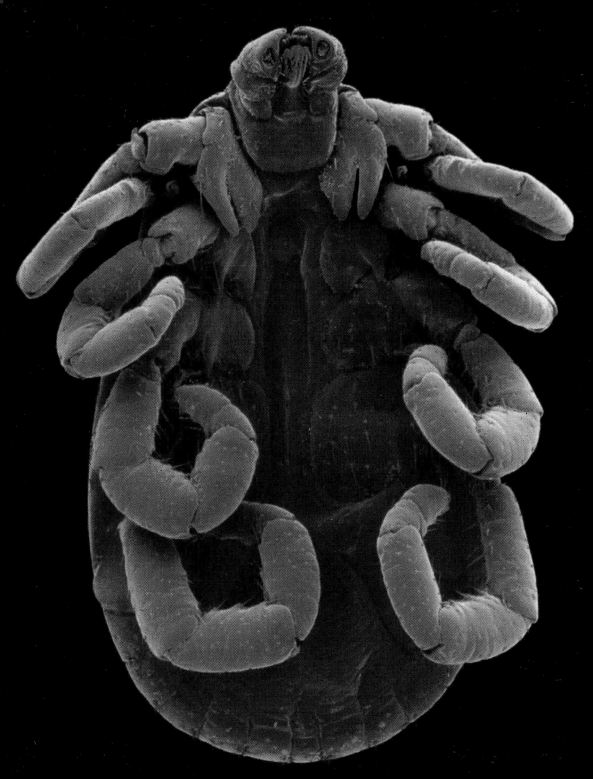

OPPOSITE: S.E.M. BY DR DENNIS KUNKEL, UNIVERSITY OF HAWAII

TICKS AND MITES

Though not as common as fleas, ticks and mites are found all over the tropical and temperate world. They don't bite, like fleas; they harpoon. They dig their sharp proboscis (nose) into the cat's skin and drink the blood. Their only food and drink is cat's blood. Cats can get potentially fatal anemias, paralysis and many other diseases from ticks and mites. They may live where fleas are found and they like to hide in cracks or seams in walls wherever cats live. They are controlled the same way fleas are controlled.

The *Dermacentor variabilis* may well be the most common tick in many geographical areas, especially those areas where the climate is hot and humid. The other common ticks that affect small animals are *Rhipicephalus sanguineus*, *Ixodes* and some species of *Amblyomma*.

Most ticks have life expectancies of a week to six months, depending upon climatic conditions. They can neither jump nor fly, but they can crawl slowly and can range up to 5 metres (16 feet) to reach a sleeping or unsuspecting animal.

INTERNAL PARASITES

Most animals—fishes, birds and mammals, including cats and humans—have worms and other parasites that live inside their bodies. According to Dr Herbert R Axelrod, the fish pathologist, there are two kinds of parasites: dumb and smart. The smart parasites live in peaceful cooperation with their

---

TOXOPLASMOSIS AND PREGNANT WOMEN

Toxoplasmosis is caused by a single parasite, *Toxoplasma gondii*. Cats acquire it by eating infected prey, such as rodents or birds, or raw meat. Obviously, strictly indoor cats are at less risk of infection than cats that are permitted to roam outdoors. Symptoms include diarrhoea, listlessness, pneumonia and inflammation of the eye. Sometimes there are no symptoms. The disease can be treated with antibiotics.

The only way humans can get the disease is through direct contact with the cat's faeces. People usually don't display any symptoms, although they can show mild flu-like symptoms. Once exposed, an antibody is produced and the person builds immunity to the disease. The real danger to humans is that pregnant women can pass the parasite to the developing foetus. In this case the chances are good that the baby will be born with a major health problem and/or serious birth defects. In order to eliminate risk, pregnant women should have someone else deal with the litterbox duties or wear gloves while taking care of the litterbox and wash hands thoroughly afterwards.

Opposite page: The tick, *Dermacentor variabilis*, is one of the most common ticks found on cats. Look at the strength in its eight legs! No wonder it's hard to detach them.

INTERNAL PARASITES OF CATS

NAME	DESCRIPTION	SYMPTOMS	ACQUISTION	TREATMENT
Roundworm (*Toxocara cati* and *Toxascaris leonina*)	Large white coil-like worms 2–4 inches long, resembling small springs.	Vomiting, pot belly, respiratory problems, poor growth rate, protruding third eyelids, poor hair coat.	Ingesting infective larvae; ingesting infected mammals, birds or insects; a queen with *Toxocari cati* nursing kittens.	Anthelmintics; scrupulously clean environment (e.g. daily removal of all faeces recommended.)
Physaloptera species	1–6 inches long, attacks the wall of the stomach.	Vomiting, anorexia, melena.	Eating insects that live in soil. (e.g. May Beetles)	Diagnosed with a gastroscope-treated with pyrantel pamoate. Prevention of exposure to the intermediate hosts.
***Gordius* or Horsehair worm**	6-inch pale brown worms with stripes.	Vomiting	May ingest a worm while drinking from or contact with swimming pools and toilet bowls.	Anthelmintics; avoiding potentially infected environments.
Hookworm (*Ancylostoma tubaeforme*)	The adult worms, ranging from 6 to 15 mm in length, attach themselves to the small intestines	Anemia, melena, weight loss, poor hair coat.	Larva penetrating the cat's skin, usually attacks the small intestine. Found in soil and flower gardens where feacal matter is deposited.	Fortnightly treatment with anthelmintics. Good sanitation (e.g. daily cleanup of litter boxes).
Tapeworm (*Dipylidium caninum* and *Taenia taeniformis*)	Up to 3 feet long. Parts shaped similar to cucumber seeds. The most common intermediate hosts are fleas and biting lice.	No clinical signs—difficult to detect.	Eating injected adult fleas. Uses rodents as hosts.	Praziquantel and epsiprantel. Management of environment to ensure scrupulously clean conditions. Proper flea control.

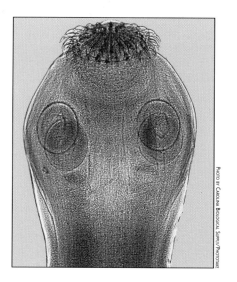

hosts (symbiosis), while the dumb parasites kill their host. Most of the worm infections are relatively easy to control. If they are not controlled they weaken the host cat to the point that other medical problems occur, but they are not dumb parasites.

HOOKWORMS
The worm *Ancylostoma tubaeforme* can inject a cat by larva penetrating its skin. It attaches itself to the small intestine of the cat where it sucks blood. This loss of blood could cause iron-deficiency anaemia.

Outdoor cats that spend much of their time in the garden or in contact with soil are commonly injected with hookworm. There is another worm, the *Gordius* or horsehair worm that, if ingested by cats, causes vomiting.

DEWORMING
Ridding your kitten of worms is VERY IMPORTANT because certain worms that kittens carry, such as tapeworms and roundworms, can infect humans.

Breeders initiate a deworming programme at or about four weeks of age. The routine is repeated every two or three weeks until the kitten is three months old. The breeder from whom you obtained your kitten should provide you with the complete details of the deworming programme.

Your veterinary surgeon can prescribe and monitor the programme of deworming for you. The usual programme is treating the kitten every 15–20 days until the kitten is positively worm free.

It is advised that you only treat your kitten with drugs that are recommended professionally.

The head and rostellum (the round prominence on the scolex) of a tapeworm, which infects cats and humans.

TAPEWORMS
There are many species of tapeworms. They are carried by fleas! The cat eats the flea and starts the tapeworm cycle. Humans can also be infected with tapeworms, so don't eat fleas! Fleas are so small that your cat could pass them onto your hands, your plate or your food and thus make it possible for you to ingest a flea which is carrying tapeworm eggs.

While tapeworm infection is not

Magnified heartworm larvae, *Dirofilaria immitis*.

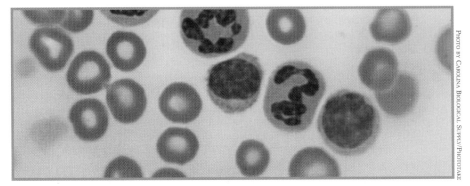

Photo by Carolina Biological Supply/Phototake

The heartworm, *Dirofilaria immitis*.

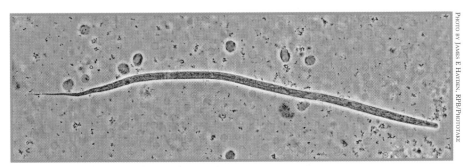

Photo by James F. Hayden, RPB/Phototake

life threatening in cats (smart parasite!), it can be the cause of a very serious liver disease for humans. About 50 percent of the humans infected with *Echinococcus multilocularis*, a type of tapeworm that causes alveolar hydatis, perish.

HEARTWORMS

Heartworms are thin, extended worms up to 30 cms (12 ins) long which are difficult to diagnose in cats as the worms are too few to be identified by the antigen-detection test. Symptoms may be loss of energy, loss of appetite, coughing, the development of a pot belly and anaemia. Heartworm injection in cats should be treated very seriously as it is often fatal.

Heartworms are transmitted by mosquitoes. The mosquito drinks the blood of an infected cat and takes in larvae with the blood. It takes two to three weeks for the larvae to develop to the infective stage within the body of the mosquito. Cats are less frequently injected with heartworms than dogs are. Also, the parasite is more likely to attack the cat's brain or other organ rather than the heart. Cats should be treated at about six weeks of age, and maintained on a prophylactic dose given monthly.

First Aid at a Glance

BURNS/SCALDS
Place the affected area under cool water; use ice if only a small area is burnt. Do not cover the burn or clip hair away. Petroleum jelly can be applied; take cat to vet immediately.

BEE/INSECT BITES
Apply freshly sliced onion. Apply ice to relieve swelling; antihistamine dosed properly.

ANIMAL BITES
Clean any bleeding area; apply pressure until bleeding subsides; go to the vet.

SPIDER BITES
Use cold compress and a pressurised pack to inhibit venom's spreading.

ANTIFREEZE POISONING
Induce vomiting with hydrogen peroxide. Seek *immediate* veterinary help!

FISH HOOKS
Removal best handled by vet; hook must be cut in order to remove.

SNAKE BITES
Pack ice around bite; contact vet quickly; identify snake for proper antivenin.

ASPHYXIA
Cat must breathe fresh air as soon as possible. Encourage your cat to move around.

CHEMICAL BURNS
Wash with water only. If you know the chemical is acid, a weak solution of sodium bicarbonate will help, or a vinegar solution will do for alkaline burns.

AUTOMOBILE ACCIDENT
Move cat from roadway with blanket; seek veterinary aid.

SHOCK
Calm the cat, keep him warm and in a horizontal position; seek immediate veterinary aid.

NOSEBLEED
Apply cold compress to the nose; apply pressure to any visible abrasion.

BLEEDING
Apply pressure above the area; treat wound by applying a cotton pack.

HEAT STROKE
Move animal to cool, shaded area, wet animal with water and place ice packs around head and body; seek immediate veterinary aid.

FROSTBITE/HYPOTHERMIA
Warm the cat with a warm bath, electric blankets or hot water bottles.

ABRASIONS
Clean the wound and wash out thoroughly with fresh water; apply antiseptic.

Remember: an injured cat may attempt to bite a helping hand from fear and confusion. Handle your cat in a calm and gentle manner so as to avoid upsetting the animal further.

THE GERIATRIC CAT

Depending on lifestyle, most cats are considered old at 12 years of age. Some problems that are associated with cats in their senior years are:

- Decreased energy
- Intolerance to heat and cold
- Less meticulous grooming and litterbox habits
- Decrease in mental alertness
- Decline of liver and kidney functions
- Greater susceptibility to diseases, especially dental disease
- Increased occurrence of cancer

As long as owners pay attention and adjust for changing behaviour and diet and continue regular veterinary care, cats can live well into their teens— some even 20 years and older!

WHAT TO DO WHEN THE TIME COMES

You are never fully prepared to make a rational decision about putting your cat to sleep. It is very obvious that you love your Persian or you would not be reading this book. Putting a loved cat to sleep is extremely difficult. It is a decision that must be made with your veterinary surgeon. You are usually forced to make the decision when your beloved pet will only suffer more and experience no enjoyment for the balance of its life. Then euthanasia is the right choice.

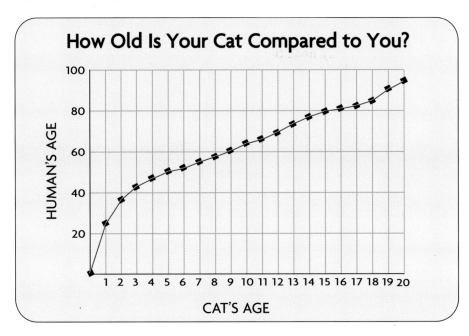

How Old Is Your Cat Compared to You?

HUMAN'S AGE

CAT'S AGE

WHAT IS EUTHANASIA?

Euthanasia derives from the Greek meaning *good death.* In other words, it means the planned, painless killing of a cat suffering from a painful, incurable condition, or who is so aged that it cannot walk, see, eat or control its excretory functions.

Euthanasia is usually accomplished by injection with an overdose of an anaesthesia or barbiturate. Aside from the prick of the needle, the experience is usually painless.

MAKING THE DECISION

The decision to euthanise your cat is never easy. The days during which the cat becomes ill and the end occurs can be unusually stressful for you. If this is your first experience with the death of a loved one, you may need the comfort dictated by your religious beliefs. If you are the head of the family and have children, you should have involved them in the decision of putting your Persian to sleep. Usually your cat can be maintained on drugs for a few days in order to give you ample time to make a decision. During this time, talking with members of your family or even people who have lived through this same experience can ease the burden of your inevitable decision.

THE FINAL RESTING PLACE

Cats can have some of the same privileges as humans. The remains of your beloved cat can be buried in a pet cemetery, which is generally expensive. Cats who have died at home can be buried in your garden in a place suitably marked with some stone or newly planted tree or bush. Alternatively, they can be cremated individually and the ashes returned to you. A less expensive option is mass cremation, although, of course, the ashes can not then be returned. Vets can usually arrange the cremation on your behalf. The cost of these options should always be discussed frankly and openly with your veterinary surgeon.

The remains of your beloved cat can be buried in a pet cemetery.

HOMEOPATHY:
an alternative to conventional medicine

'Less is Most'

Using this principle, the strength of a homeopathic remedy is measured by the number of serial dilutions that were undertaken to create it. The greater the number of serial dilutions, the greater the strength of the homeopathic remedy. The potency of a remedy that has been made by making a dilution of 1 part in 100 parts (or 1/100) is 1c or 1cH. If this remedy is subjected to a series of further dilutions, each one being 1/100, a more dilute and stronger remedy is produced. If the remedy is diluted in this way six times, it is called 6c or 6cH. A dilution of 6c is 1 part in 1000,000,000,000. In general, higher potencies in more frequent doses are better for acute symptoms and lower potencies in more infrequent doses are more useful for chronic, long-standing problems.

CURING OUR CATS NATURALLY

Holistic medicine means treating the whole animal as a unique, perfect living being. Generally, holistic treatments do not suppress the symptoms that the body naturally produces, as do most medications prescribed by conventional doctors and vets. Holistic methods seek to cure disease by regaining balance and harmony in the patient's environment. Some of these methods include use of nutritional therapy, herbs, flower essences, aromatherapy, acupuncture, massage, chiropractic, and, of course the most popular holistic approach, homeopathy. Homeopathy is a theory or system of treating illness with small doses of substances which, if administered in larger quantities, would produce the symptoms that the patient already has. This approach is often described as 'like cures like.' Although modern veterinary medicine is geared toward the 'quick fix,' homeopathy relies on the belief that, given the time, the body is able to heal itself and return to its natural, healthy state.

Choosing a remedy to cure a problem in our cats is the difficult part of homeopathy. Consult with your veterinary surgeon for a professional diagnosis of your cat's symptoms. Often these symptoms

require immediate conventional care. If your vet is willing, and somewhat knowledgeable, you may attempt a homeopathic remedy. Be aware that cortisone prevents homeopathic remedies from working. There are hundreds of possibilities and combinations to cure many problems in cats, from basic physical problems such as excessive moulting, fleas or other parasites, fever, severe skin problems, upset tummy, dry, oily or dull coat, diarrhoea, ear problems or eye discharge (including tears and dry or mucousy matter), to behavioural abnormalities, such as fear of loud noises, hypersensitivity to pain, poor appetite, aversion to touch, obesity and various phobias. From alumina to zincum metallicum, the remedies span the planet and the imagination…from flowers and weeds to chemicals, insect droppings, table salt and volcanic ash.

Using 'Like to Treat Like'

Unlike conventional medicines that suppress symptoms, homeopathic remedies treat illnesses with small doses of substances that, if administered in larger quantities, would produce the symptoms that the patient already has. Whilst the same homeopathic remedy can be used to treat different symptoms in different cats, here are some interesting remedies and their uses.

Apis Mellifica
(made from honey bee venom) can be used for allergies or to reduce swelling that occurs in acutely infected kidneys.

Calcarea Fluorica
(made from calcium fluoride which helps harden bone structure) can be useful in treating hard lumps in tissues.

Kali Muriaticum
(made from potassium chloride) can help improve sluggish behaviour.

Natrum Muriaticum
(made from common salt, sodium chloride) is useful in treating thin, thirsty cats.

Nitricum Acidum
(made from nitric acid) is used for symptoms you would expect to see from contact with acids such as lesions, especially where the skin joins the linings of body orifices or openings such as the lips and nostrils.

Symphytum
(made from the herb Knitbone, Symphytum officianale) is used to encourage bones to heal.

Urtica Urens
(made from the common stinging nettle) is used in treating painful, irritating rashes.

HOMEOPATHIC REMEDIES FOR YOUR CAT

Symptom/Ailment	Possible Remedy
ABSCESSES	Ferrum Phosphoricum 1.5c, Ledum 1.5c, Echinacea Angustifolia, Silicea 3c
ALLERGIES	Apis Mellifica 30c, Astacus Fluviatilis 6c, Pulsatilla 30c, Urtica Urens 6c
ALOPECIA	Alumina 30c, Lycopodium 30c, Sepia 30c, Thallium 6c
BLADDER PROBLEMS	Thlaspi Bursa Pastoris, Urtica Urens 3c, Apis Mellifica 1.5c, Rhus Toxicodendron 3c
CONSTIPATION	Alumina 6c, Carbo Vegetabilis 30c, Graphites 6c, Nitricum Acidum 30c, Silicea 6c
COUGHING	Aconitum Napellus 6c, Belladonna 30c, Hyoscyamus Niger 30c, Phosphorus 30c
DIARRHOEA	Arsenicum Album 30c, Aconitum Napellus 6c, Chamomilla 30c, Mercurius Corrosivus 30c
DRY EYE	Zincum Metallicum 30c
EAR MITES	Thyme (Thymus Vulgaris), Rosemary (Rosemarinus Officinalis), Rue (Ruta Gravedens)
EAR PROBLEMS	Aconitum Napellus 30c, Belladonna 30c, Hepar Sulphuris 30c, Tellurium 30c, Psorinum 200c
EYE PROBLEMS	Borax 6c, Aconitum Napellus 30c, Graphites 6c, Staphysagria 6c, Thuja Occidentalis 30c
FVR (Feline Viral Rhinotracheitis)	Ferrum Phosphoricum 3c, Kali Muriaticum 3c, Natrum Muriaticum 3c, Calcarea Phosphorica 3c
GLAUCOMA	Aconitum Napellus 30c, Apis Mellifica 6c, Phosphorus 30c
HEAT STROKE	Belladonna 30c, Gelsemium Sempervirens 30c, Sulphur 30c
HICCOUGHS	Cinchona Deficinalis 6c
INCONTINENCE	Argentum Nitricum 6c, Causticum 30c, Conium Maculatum 30c, Pulsatilla 30c, Sepia 30c
INSECT BITES	Apis Mellifica 30c, Cantharis 30c, Hypericum Perforatum 6c, Urtica Urens 30c
ITCHING	Alumina 30c, Arsenicum Album 30c, Carbo Vegetabilis 30c, Hypericum Perforatum 6c, Mezerium 6c, Sulphur 30c
LIVER PROBLEMS	Natrum Sulphuricum 1.5c, Bryonia 3c
MASTITIS	Apis Mellifica 30c, Belladonna 30c, Urtica Urens 1m
PENIS PROBLEMS	Aconitum Napellus 30c, Hepar Sulphuris Calcareum 30c, Pulsatilla 30c, Thuja Occidentalis 6c
RINGWORM	Plantago Major, Hydrastis Canadensis, Lavendula Vera, Sulphur 3c
UNDERWEIGHT CATS	Medicago Sativa, Calcarea Phosphorica 3c
VOMITING	Ipecac Root 1.5c, Ferrum Phosphoricum 3c

Recognising a Sick Cat

Unlike colicky babies and cranky children, our feline charges cannot tell us when they are feeling ill. Therefore, there are a number of signs that owners can identify to know that their cats are not feeling well.

Take note for physical manifestations such as:

- unusual, bad odour, including bad breath
- excessive moulting
- wax in the ears, chronic ear irritation
- oily, flaky, dull haircoat
- mucous, tearing or similar discharge in the eyes
- fleas or mites
- mucous in stool, diarrhoea
- sensitivity to petting or handling
- licking at paws, scratching face, etc.

Keep an eye out for behavioural changes as well including:

- lethargy, idleness
- lack of patience or general irritability
- lack of appetite, digestive problems
- phobias (fear of people, loud noises, etc.)
- strange behaviour, suspicion, fear
- coprophagia
- whimpering, crying

Get Well Soon

You don't need a DVR or a BVMA to provide good TLC to your sick or recovering cat, but you do need to pay attention to some details that normally wouldn't bother him. The following tips will aid Kitty's recovery and get him back on his paws again:

- Keep his space free of irritating smells, like heavy perfumes and air fresheners.
- Rest is the best medicine! Avoid harsh lighting that will prevent your cat from sleeping. Shade him from bright sunlight during the day and dim the lights in the evening.
- Keep the noise level down. Animals are more sensitive to sound when they are sick.

- Be attentive to any necessary temperature adjustments. A cat with a fever needs a cool room and cold liquids. A queen that is birthing or recovering from surgery will be more comfortable in a warm room, consuming warm liquids and food.
- You wouldn't send a sick child back to school early, so don't rush your cat back into a full routine until he seems absolutely ready.

USEFUL ADDRESSES

GREAT BRITAIN
The Governing Council of the Cat Fancy (GCCF)
4-6 Penel Orlieu, Bridgwater, Somerset, TA6 3PG
Email: GCCF_CATS@compuserve.com   Fax: 01278 446627 Tel: 01278 427575

The Cat Association of Britain
Mill House, Letcombe Regis, Oxon OX12 9JD   Tel: 01235-766-543

EUROPE
Federation Internationale Feline (FIFe)
Gen. Sec: Ms Penelope Bydlinski.
Little Dene, Lenham Heath, Maidstone, Kent ME17 2BS, GB
Email: penbyd@compuserve.com   Fax: 1622 850193 Tel: 1622 850908

World Cat Federation
Hubertsrabe 280, D-45307, Essen, Germany
Email: wcf@nrw-online.de   Fax: 201-552747 Tel: 201-555724

AUSTRALIA
The Australian Cat Federation, Inc.
PO Box 3305, Port Adelaide, SA 5015
Email: acf@catlover.com   Fax: 08 8242 2767 Tel: 08 8449 5880

CANADA
Canadian Cat Association
220 Advance Boulevard, Suite 101, Brampton, Ontario L6T 4J5
Email: office@cca-afc.com   Fax: 99050 459-4023 Tel: 99060459-1481

SOUTH AFRICA
Cat Federation of Southern Africa
PO Box 25, Bromhof 2154, Gauteng Province, Republic of South Africa

USA
American Cat Association
8101 Katherine Avenue, Panorama City, CA 91402
Fax: (818) 781-5340 Tel: (818) 781-5656

American Cat Fanciers Association
PO Box 203, Point Lookout, MO 65726
Email: info@acfacat.com   Fax: (417) 334-5540 Tel: (417) 334-5430

Cat Fanciers Association, Inc.
PO Box 1005, Manasquan, NJ 08736-0805
Email: cfa@cfainc.org   Fax: (732) 528-7391 Tel: (732) 528-9797

Cat Fanciers Federation
PO Box 661, Gratis, OH 45330
Email: Lalbert933@aol.com Fax: 937-787-4290 Tel: (937) 787-9009

The International Cat Association
PO Box 2684, Harlingen, Texas 78551
Email: ticaeo@xanadu2.net Tel: (956) 428-8046